CHILD COUNSELLING AND EDUCATION

CHILD COUNSELLING AND EDUCATION

(In 2 Volumes)

Child Education

(Volume-1)

V.C. Pandey

ISHA BOOKS
DELHI-110 033

Child Counselling and Education

Rs. 1800 (Set)
Rs. 900 (each volume)

ISBN: 81-8205-101-0 (Set)
ISBN: 81-8205-102-9 (Vol. 1)

Reprinted in 2018 in India by

Published in 2004 in India by
Isha Books, D-43, Prithviraj Road,
Adarsh Nagar, Delhi-110 033

First Published in 2004 in India by

Contents

Preface

The north Indian region comprises the states of Haryana, Himachal Pradesh, Jammu and Kashmir, Punjab, Rajasthan and the Union Territories of Chandigarh and Delhi. The cultural heritage of this region is an ancient and dynamic entity, spanning back to the very beginnings of human origin. It was a region that hosted one of the earliest human civilizations known as the Indus valley civilization. World's renowned great religions like Hinduism, Sikhism, Jainism are originated and flourished here.

The rich and fertile land of the north India was the meeting ground of different people and races. Its population descends from various stocks and consists of heterogeneous racial elements. Each state of the region has its own distinct tradition of art, culture, dance, music and life styles. The numerous fairs and festivals celebrated by these communities and their friendly nature are irresistible attractions for the visitors.

The region has a glorious past. It witnessed the growth and fall of various dynasties like Mauryas, the Sungas, the Yavanas, the Sakas, the Pallavas, the Kusanas, the Satavahanas, the Mugals, the Sikhs and finally the Britishers. The contribution of this land and its people to India's freedom struggle is remarkable. The national capital territory of Delhi is situated in North India.

The book offers comprehensive information on the variegated traditional religious beliefs, cultural practices and the diverse historical events in the life of people of north India. This work will prove highly informative to students, researchers, teachers and general public alike.

Editor

1

Early Childhood Care and Education

There is growing recognition of the importance of ECCE for 3-5 year olds and some emerging understanding of the importance of programmes for the under 3s. However, resources are very limited in these countries and the first priority is for adequate health care and nutrition, then for universal primary education, and then for attention to poverty reduction. There is only limited awareness of the importance and relevance of early childhood development for adult development or for the need for policies and programmes that are responsive to the extensive changes that are occurring in the larger society.

Given the limited knowledge parents may have concerning child development, there can be neglect of young children and insufficient cognitive, social, and physical stimulation. Even where programmes exist, there are shortages of qualified staff and opportunities for training. Moreover, traditional values prevail, placing a stress on care giving of very young children by mothers or by other family members when mothers are in paid, out-of-home employment and unable to provide care themselves.

The combination of traditional values, limited resources, and few qualified staff re-enforce the conventional and historic pattern of ECCE as two programs, one providing "care" to the under 3s (on a very limited basis and assuming a primary role for parents and families), and a second, providing "education" for those aged 3 to compulsory school entry largely involving a part-day program. There is not, as yet a holistic and integrated "care and education" program. This division is re-enforced further through the divided (and sometimes overlapping) policy and program responsibilities between ministries of health and social welfare with regard to care, and education with regard to preschool.

This chapter focuses on the Early childhood care and education (ECCE) programmes in developing countires giving the examples from South-East Asian countries. The countries covered are: Cambodia, Indonesia, Laos, Malaysia, Philippines, Thailand, and Vietnam.

Family Support Policies

All the ASEAN countries stress the central and traditional role of the family in rearing and socializing children. Quoting from a 1994 UN report (Declaration of Social Progress in Development), the Vietnam background country report states that "Family is a basic unit of society and a natural environment for development and happiness for all family members, particularly the children." It goes on to state that "From time immemorial all ethnic groups in the Southeast Asian Region have been greatly influenced by oriental philosophies, the most influential of all is the philosophy originating from Confucianism". Respect for the elderly is a repeated theme, as is support for multi-generational and extended families.

Although each of the countries in the region has its own culture and even some communities have different philosophies, the value placed on the traditional family is a shared value throughout the region. Yet despite this, as indicated earlier and in all the background country reports, present day families are experiencing significant changes due to the impact of economic development, demographic, social, and cultural change.

The changes have brought about some important positive results (improved health, reduced income poverty, extended and enhanced education, reduced gender inequities) but also have led to changes in the relationship between families and society, especially with regard to the education, socialization, and care of young children; and inequities remain and have even increased between urban and rural areas.

Improvement in the status and role of women is a fundamental component of any effort towards enhancing the situation of children, as has been discussed above, and is a repeated theme in the background country reports. Legislative initiatives targeted on this goal occurred in all of these countries over the last two decades.

Paralleling and supplementing these initiatives are women, child and family-related laws enacted in several of these countries, often influenced by the 1990 World Summit on Children and the enactment of the UN Convention on the Rights of the Child. For example, a law on marriage and the family enacted in 1959 in Vietnam, was amended in 1986 and again in 2000, stipulating individual's rights and obligations regarding marriage. Two important laws enacted in 1991 are the Law on Child Protection and Care and the Law on Universal Primary Education establishing free public primary education.

There is growing interest now in ECCE and in ensuring access to these programs in rural as well as urban areas. There is also growing interest in enhancing parental knowledge and understanding of child development and how parents can contribute to and participate in the education of their young children.

The major provisions of the legislation directed at children and their families have to do with nutrition, health care and primary and secondary education. In addition, most of the countries have enacted laws having to do with the protection of women's and children's legal rights, especially with regard to protection against physical and sexual abuse and exploitation.

Thailand

Child and family policy is only beginning to be conceptualized as such in several of these countries. In Thailand, for example, a policy statement was issued by Prime Minister Taksin Shinawatra on February 6, 2001, stating that a primary function of government is to promote family strength and that families are the basic unit of economic development and a shelter from social problems. Among the objectives of Thailand's child and family policy announced in his statement are:

1. to establish community-based centers for providing information, advice, and help to families with regard to health care and family planning;
2. to support quality, community-based, pre-primary schools;
3. to protect children against abuse and punish those who violate or abuse children;

4. to promote women's rights, status, roles, and gender equity.

The policy so stated conforms to the provisions of the Eighth National Economic and Social Development Plan (1997-2001) and includes: a redefinition of the minimum age for children to enter paid employment, from 13 to 15; an enhanced law concerning the disabled; a new National Education Act (1999) extending basic education to 12 years; provision for expanded opportunities for NGOs, civic groups, and other social institutions to participate in educational issues; protection of women and children with regard to prostitution; plans for the enactment in 2010 for legislation regarding the Youth Family Court and Youth Rehabilitation Center.

The Thai concept is that government, NGOs, and the private sector should work together in order to achieve child and youth protection generally. Only limited data and evidence exist, however, with regard to the implementation and enforcement of these laws. Nonetheless, child well-being did improve during the 1990s. For example, infant mortality rates declined significantly from 8.0 per thousand live births in 1950 to 5.8 in 1997. Thailand has enacted a paid and job-protected maternity leave at the time of childbirth, lasting 90 days and replacing 50 percent of prior wages. A lump sum cash benefit is also provided, for one birth.

It is estimated that the Royal Thai government invests about 3.9 percent of GDP on children and youth, with the largest portion spent on education. Primary education is compulsory in Thailand but at least 10 percent of children could still not access school at the end of the 1990s. Sixty percent of sixth graders do not go on to secondary school.

Traffic accidents are the leading cause of death among youth aged 15-24 and risk behaviors such as smoking, drinking alcohol, drug addiction, teen-out-of-wedlock pregnancy and births, are significant problems. Half of the 13-14 year olds are already in the labor market and half of those working are in the family-agriculture sector. It is estimated that with the HIV/AIDS epidemic and the economic problems of the late 1990s, child abuse, child neglect, child prostitution, and child labor are likely to increase.

Malaysia

Following the World Summit for Children in 1990, a document entitled "Caring for the Children of Malaysia – A National Plan of Action for Child Survival, Protection, and Development" was drawn up by an inter-ministerial committee with representation from NGOs and was approved by the Cabinet in 1994. This served as the blueprint for the development and formulation of policies, strategies, and programs for children up to the year 2000.

Relevant legislation in Malaysia includes several acts concerning the juvenile courts, adoption legislation enacted in 1952 and revised in 1981, a child labor act passed in 1966, a women and girls' protection act passed in 1973 and revised in 1987, and child protection and child care acts passed in 1981 and the 1990s. Malaysia has enacted childbirth-related leaves including a 60-day, paid and jobprotected maternity leave for working women following childbirth and three days paid and job-protected paternity leave.

Several child-conditioned tax benefits have been established including a child benefit, a child maintenance benefit, a tax benefit to offset some of the costs to parents of education and medical expenses, tax benefits to employers in the private sector for the cost of building child care centers at the workplace. In response to the rising labor force participation rates of women, policies have been established encouraging flexible work schedules and teleworking to help women manage work and family life. Among the policies recommended for the future, is the establishment of a social impact statement for all new development projects.

Indonesia

In Indonesia, the development of children is viewed as part of the effort to improve the quality of human resources in the country. Policies and programs currently conducted to support families include: poverty alleviation through community empowerment strategies; provision of credit and finance schemes; family planning services; a Safe Motherhood program and promotion of a program that involves the responsibility of husbands; policies designed to improve nutrition, health status, and education of children including the establishment of community-based health services for young children aged 3-6; increasing the legal protection of children; policies designed to increase the role of the family and community in the care of children.

Several government agencies in collaboration with international agencies such as the World Bank, the Asian Development Bank, UNICEF, and others responded to the economic crisis of 1997 by providing support for two major programs for children including food and nutrition programs and access to public health and education. In addition, a consortium of NGOs and community groups established a Community Recovery Program to empower local communities to assist the poorest and most vulnerable population affected by the crisis. Some private corporations contributed as well.

During the period of 1992-1997, the number of working children 10-15 years of age decreased from 2.3 to 1.6 million or proportionately from 10.2 to 7.4 percent. However, the decline was greater for boys (9.4 percent) than girls (6.9 percent). The official age for compulsory education is 6-12 for primary education and 13-15 for secondary education, for a total of 9 years of compulsory education. However, there are no data provided about actual enrollment and coverage.

Indonesia is seeking to strengthen child and family caring practices. The program includes promoting home visits and home-based activities that support safe pregnancies and deliveries, promote breast feeding and birth spacing, protect young children against abuse, provide early psychological stimulation as well as helping parents avoid developmental delays among young children. Attention is paid to improving women's health and their education as a strategy for enhancing the development of children. The scale of implementation is not reported.

The Philippines

Article II in the Philippines constitution covers several relevant aspects of child and family policy, for example: an explicit recognition of the family as the basic social institution; the natural and primary right and duty of parents in the rearing of children; the roles of children, youth, and women in nation building; equality of women and men; the protection and promotion of the right of all to health care; education as a priority; the rights of indigenous minorities

Very young children (under 6) are considered especially vulnerable to the consequences of poverty, infant mortality rates are viewed as too high (35 per 1000 births), and anemia and wasting are considered to be major problems. The Philippines also provide a paid maternity leave for 60 days, covered by a cash benefit replacing 100 percent of prior wages.

Cambodia

Education is at the heart of child and family policies in Cambodia. The system of education in Cambodia is divided into preschool for 3 to 5 year olds, primary school for children aged 6 to 12, lower secondary school (grades 7,8,9), upper secondary school (grades 10,11,12), vocational training schools, and higher education.

In 1996-97 the 12 year system of education was established with the government expected to provide 9 years of free education for all under the aegis of the Ministry of Education, Youth, and Sport (MOEYS) Only 60 percent of 5-17 year olds attend school full time now. The main current focus is on implementing the policy already announced and improving the quality of that education.

In recent years, especially since the enactment of the UN Convention on the Rights of the Child in 1990, most of these countries have enacted legislation providing for the protection of children and women. Attention to and concern about children have increased, with particular attention placed on confirming the centrality of the family while acknowledging family and gender role changes, the link between women's status and child well-being, and the need for more attention to children.

ECCE Policies and Programmes

The trends influencing the growing demand for ECCE include:

— The increasing number and percentage of women in the labor force, especially those with young children.

— The decline of the extended family and increase of nuclear families. The increasing awareness of the importance of preparing children for primary school.

— The ratification of the United Nations Convention on the Rights of the Child (UNCRC).

— The World Summit for Children, held in 1990.

— The need for alternative, affordable childcare.

— The need to ensure access to primary and secondary school, especially for the girl child.

— Continued relatively high birth rates producing a large population of young children.

— The multi-ethnic nature of the population requiring a common, shared experience to prepare them for primary school.

— The problem of street children especially in Vietnam, Indonesia, Laos, and Cambodia and their need to be prepared for school and to be socialized into the society.

The obstacles to expanding ECCE include: the competition for resources with other needs such as reducing poverty, increasing access to health care, coping with natural disasters, and the lack of trained ECCE staff. Most importantly, the obstacles include as well the administrative arrangements within government for setting policies and implementing them, and the extent to which care and education are viewed as integrated – and administered under one government agency – or separate and administered by several agencies, departments, or ministries. The country "cases" which follow vary in content and length, with the countries that have the most significant developments receiving the most attention.

Thailand

In Thailand, school-aged children receive far more policy and program attention than preschoolers. Most parents lack the knowledge of child development needed to bring up their very young children adequately and do not understand young children's development from birth through five years of age, or the link between the preschool experience and subsequent child outcomes. Communities have limited resources and limited interest in developing ECCE programs. Health care is a priority and the supply of ECCE centers is very inadequate. What is there, is for 3-5 year olds, administered under the auspices of the Ministry of Education.

Four major governmental agencies are involved in providing the very limited care for children aged 0-3: Ministries of Education, Public Health, University Affairs, and Interior. UNICEF and several NGOs are also involved.

Since the declaration of the current Constitution (1997) people have been exposed to new ideas about child and youth development and have begun to appreciate the importance of early childhood for adult development. Among the more recent initiatives are:

— Reform of both formal and informal education;

— Early childhood initiatives begun in 1964 and coordinated by the Council for Children and Youth Development;

— Health care reform, including attention to HIV/AIDS infected mothers and children;

— A civil society movement that aims at strengthening families and communities;

— The movement of community organizations, NGOs and civic groups working to achieve specific targets having to do with improving the situation of disadvantaged children and families;

Research studies carried out by the Child Welfare Association in Thailand. A UNICEF-funded programme operated from 1987 to 1998 with the involvement of seven organizations: the Ministries of Education, Public Health, University Affairs, and Interior, and several Thai NGOs. It focused on teaching parents about child development and nurturing. A second programme, serving 3-5 year olds, called "Learning Reform of Early Childhood Education: Student Centered Approach" is being piloted from 1999 to 2002 under the Office of the National Education Commission, Office of the Prime Minister. Its focus is on the establishment of public and private ECCE programs. A teacher-training programme is being piloted during these same years for these programmes.

Despite a miscellany of ad hoc ECCE initiatives, there is no clear picture regarding coverage of preschool-aged children in ECCE centers in Thailand. A 1996-97 survey revealed that 54.2 percent of these children nationwide were cared for at home while 37.3 percent were enrolled in centers. Generally, children were cared for by their mothers (53.1 percent) or relatives (19.7 percent) but there seems to be some overlap in these figures.

Apart from the inadequate supply of ECCE programmes, some other early childhood problems include:

— Parental ignorance of the factors impeding or enhancing early child development, especially among families living in rural areas;

— The lack of resources in local communities and rural areas for establishing programs providing cognitive, social, physical stimulation;

— Inadequate recognition of the importance of the early years (0-5) in the Thai society.

Only since the 1997 Constitution have people begun to understand the importance of children and youth to the society at large. Thus, there is some beginning attention to educational reform and lifelong learning, health care reform including special attention to HIV/AIDS infected mothers and children, and civil society developments with special attention to children.

During 1977-2001 several programmatic initiatives for children and families were launched, coordinated by the Council for Children and Youth Development. These included: ECCE initiatives; child welfare initiatives; and protection of children's rights across different systems. Most of these initiatives, however, are operative only in big cities. There is still no extension to rural areas but it is expected that these areas will get more attention in the future, as will child and youth issues generally.

Malaysia

In Malaysia, the care of preschool aged children comes under the responsibility of a large number of government departments and social agencies such as the Ministry of Health, Ministry of National Unity and Social Development, Ministry of Rural Development; and the several state departments.

Following the World Summit for Children in 1990, the report, Caring for the Children of Malaysia –National Plan of Action for Child Survival, Protection and Development was prepared and approved by the Cabinet in 1994. This served as the blueprint for the development and formulation of policies, programs, and strategies for children up to the year 2000.

Malaysia has achieved its goals for primary education (and for safe water and sanitation and for childhood immunization). The national target of 100 percent primary school participation was achieved by 1994. Basic primary education is free and universal and covers all children even though it is not compulsory.

Almost all children in the primary grades are in grades appropriate for their age. The transition rate between grades in primary school averaged 99.8 percent in 1994 and the rate of enrolment from primary to secondary school was 91.2 percent and from lower secondary to upper secondary, 85.7. These rates are impressive, especially given that although free, school is not compulsory in Malaysia; but clearly it is highly valued, and coupled with universal access can lead to full coverage. There are also primary schools for children with special needs.

There is equality in access to education opportunities by gender. In 1997 the proportion of female enrollment in public primary schools was 51.5 percent, in lower secondary schools, 50.5 percent, and in upper secondary schools, 47.5 percent. Technical and vocational schools are still dominated by males (67 percent) but females constitute almost half of the University students, 47.5 percent.

The focus now is on enhancing quality of education by way of updating curriculum and strengthening basic skills in reading, writing, and mathematics. According to the Malaysian country report Education For All: The Year 2000 Assessment (1999), ECCE programs are divided into home-based centers (what some would call family day care homes) serving fewer than 10 children and targeted largely on children under age 4, and preschools for 4-6 year olds, disproportionately available in urban areas. The objectives for the preschools include: providing care for the children of working parents; providing employment opportunities for women; stimulating broader societal support for ECCE; providing cognitive, social, physical and spiritual stimulation for children; preparing children for primary school.

Preschool education is conducted largely by the government, and then by NGOs, and other private social organizations. The government operated 81.6 percent of the preschool programs in 1995. Of these, 61.8 percent are operated by the Community Development Division of the Ministry of Rural Development, 9.5 percent by the Ministry of National Unity and Social Development, and 10.3 percent by the Ministry of Education. The other 18.4

percent are operated by the private sector. Public preschool programs are free to parents and fully funded by the government. Private programs charge fees.

Coverage for preschool education has improved dramatically over the last decadeand-one-half, from 17 percent of 4-6 year olds in 1981 to 41.5 percent in 1995. The goal was 65 percent by the year 2000. However, the Malaysian report notes that in comparison with the full and universal coverage of primary school education, there is need for further improvement.

It is expected that the 1996 Education Act will be amended to make preschool as well as primary school compulsory. The focus now is on expanding preschool programs with a particular stress on stimulating cognitive, physical and socio-emotional development. A Cabinet Committee has been formed comprising the Ministries of Education, National Unity and Social Development, and Rural Development with the goal of enabling all preschool-aged children to participate. One problem in moving towards universal preschool coverage is geographical. Part of East Malaysia can be accessed largely only by air or rivers, through heavy forest and across mountains.

Although the Ministry of Education (MOE) does not fund and operate all the preschools in Malaysia, it does have responsibility for preparing the preschool curriculum for all. It also carries out teacher training, registers preschool centers, and in general, implements preschool education.

The NGOs involved in preschools include: the Malaysian Kindergarten Association, the Malaysian Association of Child Care Providers, the Malaysian Council for Child Welfare, and the National Association of Preschool Teachers. Although preschool teachers are required to have formal training in ECCE before being permitted to teach, it is not clear how long the training is or what it consists of apart from pedagogy and educational psychology. Nor is it clear what the content of the preschool curriculum is, nor the duration of the school day and year and whether it functions as a childcare program as well.

A 1998 study of "Childcare and Parenting Styles Among Working Parents in Malaysia" conducted by the National Population and Family Development Board found that working parents rely heavily on family members for care of their young children while they work (30.6 percent) and also on themselves (14.6 percent). Among the family members, grandparents played a major role in providing childcare (60.4 percent) followed by other relatives (22.5 percent) and older siblings (17.1 percent). Neighbors and friends provided another 15 percent of the childcare. Domestic servants accounted for 6.6 percent of child care, with 68 percent of the caregivers Indonesians, while 24 percent were Malaysian and Filipinos, 5.4 percent.

Childcare centers accounted for only 5.1 percent of the care provided. However, about 18 percent of the children had no specially assigned caregivers but were under supervision at public or religious schools. Only a very few parents (1.5 percent) sent their children away from home to stay with relatives for sustained periods of time. About 9 percent of the children had no caregivers and can be considered "latch key" children, left alone by themselves while their parents worked outside of the home.

Unfortunately, the data that are provided in this study are not consistent. Nor are they desegregated by the age of the child, so it is unclear what portion of the child care is for primary school aged children, what for preschoolers and among the latter, how the care is allocated for the 0-3 year olds and for the 4-6 year olds. Nor is it clear what the content of the preschool curriculum includes nor the duration of the preschool day. Nor is the relationship between "child care" and "preschool education" clear.

Preschool teachers must attend formal training or a special course before they can teach at a kindergarten or preschool. Training is conducted at Teacher Training Colleges under the Ministry of Education or other relevant ministries and government departments. However, it is not clear how long the training is nor what it consists of. The public preschools are fully funded by the government. The government pays for all expenses including teacher salaries, capital costs and equipment, food subsidies, etc. In private preschools, parents pay fees and the other expenses are borne by the operator/caregiver.

The Malaysian government is greatly concerned about the inadequacies in its preschool programs and supportive of efforts to expand the supply of preschools, to amend the Education Act of 1996 and make preschool education compulsory, and to increase investment in preschool and education generally. It is also concerned with monitoring and enhancing the quality of the programs, increasing the supply, strengthening and expanding teacher training, and, most importantly, increasing collaboration and cooperation across the several government agencies involved.

The Malaysian government plays a major role in supporting families. It has made significant progress in the care and development of young children following earlier plans. A large number of policies and programs are already in place to ensure the well-being of children and their families, with particular attention to health care and education. Efforts are expected to continue in the 21st century to support families with children, especially with regard to the care and education of young children.

Indonesia

In Indonesia, the development of children is mostly a family-level responsibility. When parents are not able to be the primary caregivers, because of employment outside the home, care is carried out by relatives, neighbors, or care services. These ECCE services/programs are designed to optimize the survival, growth, and development of children.

There are several types of early childhood programs that focus largely on providing education and health care, but care and education are viewed as separate functions and data are not available with regard to coverage and the portion of eligible children in each program type. Only 27 percent of first graders were found to have had any prior preschool experience at the end of the 1990s.

— *Child (day) care centers* provide services for children from 3 months to six years of age who need care while their parents work outside the home. Both government and non-governmental organizations operate these centers, which are under the responsibility of the Ministry of Social Affairs while the educational supervision is provided by the Ministry of National Education since 1990. Most centers are in urban areas because, according to the report, women in rural areas prefer to leave their children in the care of other family members when they are working.

— *Playgroups are part-day (2 hours a day),* part week (3 days a week) programs that are similar to the day care centers but operate on a much more limited scale. Under the Ministries of Social Affairs and National Education, they serve the 0-3 year olds and have as their primary goal developing children's social skills and readiness for school, thus focusing on meeting children's needs rather than on the needs of working parents.

— *Kindergartens* provide early education services for children aged 4-6. Most kindergartens divide children into two groups, one for 4-5 year olds and a second for 5-6 year olds. Kindergartens operate under the authority of the Ministry of National Education.

— *Posyandu* is a type of health and nutrition, home-based service designed to encourage the psychosocial development of children aged 3-6 and is under the responsibility of the Ministry of Health. A member of the family is recruited to function as a change and development agent to provide information and advice about health and nutrition.

A "Family and Under Five Development Program" trains/educates mothers and other caregivers to help them to better stimulate children's cognitive, physical, and socio-emotional development and to monitor the child's physical growth. The government conducts training programs for kindergarten teachers and day care and playgroup providers through teacher training institutions.

According to the Indonesian report, national budget allocations for education, health, and social services are very limited and ECCE programs are under-funded at the community as well as national level. There is need for responsibility for these programs – and financing – to be shared among government, community organizations, and NGOs. There is also need for special education programs, which now are only available beginning with kindergarten, and the supply does not even meet that need.

Approximately 40 percent of working women care for their children while working, 37 percent rely on female relatives especially grandmothers, and 10 percent use older female siblings to help. In rural areas older female siblings are the primary caregivers of young children. Mothers in urban areas are more likely to use domestic help or the out-of-home care services described above.

The challenges confronting Indonesia's early childhood policy and provision include: poor health status, unequal access to health services, and low utilization of health services; widespread malnutrition among children under the age of 5; low quality and quantity of early child development care and education services; education that lacks relevance to children's needs; inadequate efforts at achieving higher status for women; sustaining its educational participation rate.

We might add that another challenge is the failure to integrate care and education. Indonesia has established a set of Broad Guidelines for State Policy that include special attention to empowering families to make and act on informed decisions regarding the care of its members including children, with regard to their health, education, care, and protection against abuse and exploitation.

The Philippines

A consistent finding in research in the Philippines is that mothers are the primary caregivers of young children, especially infants. At later ages, other family members such as grandparents and older siblings play an important role. Depending on the socioeconomic status of the family, paid, in-home caregivers are important for preschool aged children up to age 10. When children are old enough for preschool (age 3), the neighborhood childcare center or a private preschool takes care of the children for 2-3 hours a day.

Compulsory school begins at age 6 but only 86 percent of those entering primary school go from first to second grade. ECCE programs are supposed to improve this. Public childcare centers as well as public primary schools are subsidized by the local or national governments. If fees are charged, they are largely voluntary and very minimal. Parents who cannot afford the fees volunteer their services (cleaning the center or assisting staff). Parents who can afford higher fees send their children to private preschools, some of which, according to the report, charge fees that are even higher than college or university tuition.

Staff may have formal university degrees in early childhood education or family life and child development. Or, they may take short non-degree courses in community or childcare centers. Graduates of the degree programs usually work in the private childcare programs where salaries are higher.

With the passage of the Early Child Care and Development (ECCD) Law in 2000, some of the policies announced in the constitution are beginning to be implemented. The Law recognizes the importance of early childhood and its special needs, affirms parents as primary caregivers and the child's first teachers, and establishes parent effectiveness seminars and nutrition counseling for pregnant and lactating mothers.

The objectives of the National ECCD programmes include:

— improvement of infant and child survival rates through expanded child health programs; enhanced roles of parents and caregivers through parent effectiveness seminars and counseling;

— enhanced cognitive, physical, social and emotional development of young children through the establishment of additional child care centers under the Department of Social Welfare;

— a smooth transition from at-home care to pre or primary schools through a two-month bridging program for entrants to primary school;

— creating a system for early intervention and prevention of developmental problems and disabilities; enhanced capabilities of caregivers through training of child care staff;

— improvement of the quality of public and private ECCD programs through registration and accreditation of programs;

— promotion of the ECCD programmes through the establishment of linkages between local government units, the Departments of Health, Education, and Social Welfare, and the appointment of an early child development official in every city to coordinate and supervise all these activities.

The Law requires the establishment of a National Coordinating Council for the Welfare of Children which establishes guidelines, standards, and culturally relevant practices for ECCD programs; develops a national system for the recruitment, training, and accrediting of caregivers; monitors the delivery of ECCD services and the impact on beneficiaries; provides additional resources to poor and disadvantaged communities in order to increase the supply of ECCD programmes; encourages the development of private sector initiatives.

ECCD programmes include: child care programmes; parent effectiveness seminars; child minding centers; family day care services; parent-child development programmes; and kindergartens in public schools. All but the kindergartens have local government units and the Department of Social Welfare as the responsible administrative agency and funding source. Where the kindergartens are concerned, the responsible agency and funding source is the Department of Education.

The Departments of Health and Social Welfare and Development are the government agencies with primary responsibility for both the 0-3 year olds and the 3-6 year olds. They provide health care and protection against child abuse and abandonment. The Department of Education assumes responsibility only when children enter kindergarten or primary school. There are no data on the extensiveness of these programmes, the proportion of children of different ages who are served by each program, or whether there is overlap among them. One estimate of coverage is 8 percent of 0-6 year olds in some kind of program in 1998; double the rate in1990. In 1999, 71 percent of first graders did have some prior preschool experience, largely at age 5; 3 percent of these were in public programmes.

Even where ECCD programmes exist, however, the supply is limited and quality is poor. For example, two programmes that are currently operating under the Department of Social Welfare, are: (1) a 2-3 hour childcare program for 4-6 year olds; and (2) a parent effectiveness program. About 43 percent of the villages have these programs but lack resources – supplies, equipment, and qualified staff – to adequately cover all the children of this age, or their parents. According to one recent case study of ECCD programs in the Philippines, "Considering the length of time that ECCD programmes have been implemented in the Philippines, information systems for ECCD are relatively undeveloped". The biggest gap in ECCD provision is in programs for the under 3s.

Vietnam

Vietnam, like all other Southeast Asian countries, stresses the role of parents and families in providing early childhood care and education. However, in recent years it has increased attention to preschool-aged children. In 1991, a law was enacted establishing universal primary education.

In 1999, another law was enacted regarding preschool education, establishing responsibility for programs for 0-6 year olds under one ministry, that of Education and Training, and with links to the Ministry of Health and to Women's organizations. The supply of ECCE programs is inadequate in rural areas and among poor children.

Vietnam provides a paid and job-protected maternity leave for women in the paid labor force lasting 120 days and replacing 100 percent of prior wages. It covers adoption as well as childbirth. Legislation also provides for an additional unpaid leave lasting 180 days that may be provided by employers.

There are no data on the proportion of women who are covered by these leave policies at childbirth. As in many other countries, early childhood care and education policies and programs are targeted primarily on the 3-5 year olds. Eight percent of 0-3 year olds but 45 percent of 3-5 year olds have access to ECCE in Vietnam. About 76 percent of 5 year olds are enrolled in kindergarten. Access and quality vary dramatically between urban and rural areas. The supply of ECCE is clearly inadequate, but especially for the 0-3 year olds. Access in general is limited, and fees are reduced for poor children but still too high for many families. The programs are overwhelmingly public or publicly subsidized; only 1 percent is private.

ECCE policies and programs are integrated administratively under one ministry, but the delivery system still appears to be fragmented. There are nurseries for children aged 3 months to 3 years and kindergartens for 3 to 6 year olds. In addition to providing care and education for these very young children, the programs are designed to provide cognitive, physical, and social stimulation and prepare children for first grade. Current policies are aimed at increasing the supply and coverage rate in kindergarten to 70-80 percent, developing family day care homes for the under 3s, and stimulating public support and increased investment.

Vietnam is promoting an integrated administrative approach with one government Ministry, the Ministry of Education and Training, holding primary responsibility for children from birth to age 8, but it is not yet implemented. The goals are: to make parents more informed about child development and good parenting; to establish lowcost community-based programs linked with health care services; to establish safe ECCE programs; and to increase the supply of programs for the 0-3s and for the rural population. The problem of street children – often migrants from rural areas – and of orphans, require special attention as well. The current trend is to encourage the development of private ECCE programmes but the government will fund programs in the disadvantaged communities.

Cambodia

Some of the consequences of the problems listed earlier include:

(1) a reduction in the numbers of available caretakers for children;

(2) a reduction in the ability of existing caretakers to provide care; and

(3) a scarcity of resources available to caregivers to support the survival, education, and socialization of children in need of care.

The most important needs for children are nutrition, health care, education, and daily care. ECCE comes later.

In 2000 for the first time, the Ministry of Education, Youth, and Sport (MOEYS) formally articulated a "Policy on ECE" which may constitute the first step towards a national ECCE policy. Care of the 0-3 year olds is largely by mothers bringing babies to the fields while they work, or, secondarily, by older siblings.

ECCE is focused primarily on children aged 3 to compulsory school entry, technically age 6 but the policy covers children aged 3-8. These programmes are under the auspices of the MOEYS which increasingly now recognizes the importance of early childhood education for the 0-3s as well as the 3-5year olds, but has not yet made a significant move towards increasing the supply of programs. The government agency with primary responsibility for preschool is the MOEYS. The agencies with primary responsibility for the younger children (0-3) include the Ministry of Women's and Veteran's Affairs (MOWVA), the Ministry of Health and the Ministry of Rural Development. The MOWVA also has responsibility for the Early Childhood Development (ECCE in our terms) communitybased groups/centers for 0-6 year olds.

The types of formal preschools include:

— independent and free-standing public preschools;

— preschools linked to public primary schools;

— preschools linked to factories and enterprises;

— preschools linked to Cambodian NGOs and International NGOs; and private preschools (with no government support) including some for affluent families situated in well-to-do communities and others, less formal, for poor families, located in poor neighborhoods.

There are also informal community-based childcare centers.

The MOEYS and MOWVA are involved in training staff and volunteers for the government-funded/sponsored programs. There is a one-year training program for the preschool staff of MOEYS programs, carried out at a teacher training school, and short training programs provided by the MOWVA (22 days), and the international NGOs (20 days).

The supply of preschool programs is very limited and coverage is very sparse. Preschools enroll about 10 percent of the 5-6 year olds and another 25 percent of 6 year olds are in primary school. They constitute about two-thirds of all the preschoolers. About 5 percent of 3-5 year olds are also enrolled.

There is multiplicity and overlap among the government agencies with responsibility for ECCE, especially with regard to the under 3s. These agencies include the MOWVA, Health, and Rural Development for the 0-3s and MOEYS for those aged 3 to compulsory school entry. There are mechanisms established under the aegis of the MOEYS to promote and facilitate coordination across the relevant ministries but between the paucity of programmes and places for children and the multiplicity of agencies involved, the background country report does not suggest extensive cooperation or collaboration around policies, program operations, or data collection.

Laos

Compulsory school begins at age 6 and 5 years of education are required; but the policy does not seem to be enforced. After 1975, preschool education was introduced through the establishment of two types of programs (one for the under 3s and another for the 3-5 year olds) at places of work. At the end of the first 5-year plan (1981 –1985) about 3 percent of children aged 3 months to 5 years were enrolled. By 1988, coverage was a little more extensive with 2 percent coverage of the 0-3s and 8 percent of the 3-5 year olds enrolled. The rates are lower for girls. All these rates may have declined since then but there are no later data.

The ECCE objectives are similar to those identified in the other countries, in particular, (1) providing cognitive, physical, and social stimulation, and (2) preparation for primary school. The Ministry of Education has responsibility for both infant/toddler programs and preschools, along with some support from the international NGOs. The government pays the salaries of the "teachers" in these programs and there is one teacher training school in the country.

The ECCE policies and programs described in the seven countries are consistent in the goals they are trying to achieve (cognitive, physical social stimulation; enhanced child development; preparation for primary school) but clearly, not in the extent to which they have been achieved. Most countries allocate ECCE responsibility to several different agencies. Ministries of education are always one of the agencies but ministries involving social welfare, rural development, interior, or health are often involved as well, with little evidence of collaboration across agencies. Only Vietnam appear to have assigned one ministry, education, the full responsibility for ECCE while Malaysia seems to have placed education in a lead position, but not the sole position. The Philippines and Indonesia divide responsibility according to the age of the children, between two ministries, education and social affairs or health.

Framework for Action on Values Education in Early Childhood

During the 1999 UNESCO General Conference, several Member States representatives expressed their concern about young children who did not receive the proper quality of education, or were not exposed to any education at all, or were part of communities where crucial values were being eroded, and their desire to find ways in which those values can be strengthened. UNESCO receives more and more requests from Member States related to the issue of values education for young children (within a formal and non formal educational framework, but also street children, etc.). Building on this, UNESCO's Early

Childhood and Family Education Unit launched, jointly with Living Values: An Educational Programme, an international initiative on "Early Childhood and Values Education" in early 2000. This started an "international" discussion (in English, French and Spanish - by email and other traditional means) on the theme of Early Childhood and Values Education involving, among other, the distribution of a questionnaire to Living Values coordinators and educators, UNESCO National Commissions and field offices and other early childhood partners throughout the world, to identify experiences in this area, solicit recommendations on forms of concrete and practical results of such a discussion and consultation, and suggest ideas that could help prepare documents for Member States, educators, parents, etc on this issue.

Meeting basic needs

Summarized from the results of the discussions during the meeting and recent statements on young children's needs, the following findings provide a quick overview of needs that would need to account in be taken into an early childhood value-based framework for action.

Reaching young children

The *Education for All 2000 Assessment* shows that of the more than 800 million children under 6 years of age in the world, fewer than a third benefit from any form of early childhood programmes. The challenge is thus enormous, made more difficult by the demographic pressures and increased urbanization, increased poverty and social exclusion, greater numbers of out-of-school children, the alarming progress of AIDS, growing violence among youth and the impact of globalization that most countries experience. Yet, efficient and low-cost options for early childhood exist, and are adapted to the needs of children, to the living conditions of families, to the different cultures, values and resources of countries. Their implementation depends more on creating adequate political and social will, and a cohesion among the various actors in education, than on any other factor.

Irreducible needs of young children

In their new book *"The Irreducible Needs of Children"*, Doctors T. Berry Brazelton and Stanley Greenspan argue that all young children have seven irreducible needs.

1. *Ongoing nurturing relationships:* Every baby needs a warm, intimate relationship with a primary caregiver over a period of years, not months or weeks. This is far more important to emotional and intellectual development that early cognitive training or educational games. If this relationship is absent or interrupted, a child can develop disorders of reasoning, motivation and attachment. Infants, toddlers and preschoolers need these nurturing interactions most of their waking hours.
2. *Physical protection, safety and regulation*: Both in the womb and in infancy, children need an environment that provides protection from physical and psychological harm, chemical toxins and exposure to violence.
3. *Experiences tailored to individual differences:* Every child has a unique temperament. Tailoring early experience to nurture a child's individual nature prevents learning and behavioral problems and enables a child to develop his or her full potential.

4. *Developmentally appropriate experiences*: Children of different ages need care tailored to their stage of development. Unrealistic expectations can hinder a child's development.

5. *Limit-setting, structure and expectations*: Children need structure and discipline. They need discipline that leads to internal limit-setting, channelling of aggression and peaceful problem-solving. To reach this goal, they need adults who empathize as well as set limits. They need expectations rather than labels, and adults who believe in their potential but understand their weaknesses. They need incentive systems, not failure models.

6. *Stable, supportive communities and culture*: To feel whole and integrated, children need to grow up in a stable community. This means a continuity of values in family, peer groups, religion and culture, as well as an exposure to diversity.

7. *Protecting the future*: Meeting all these needs should be our highest priority. If we fail, we will jeopardize our children's future.

Early childhood and values education

Research confirms the importance of the early years to positively influence children in a long-lasting way. The value orientations of children are largely determined by the time they reach the age of formal schooling. The first steps towards a lifetime of peaceful, non-violent activities, of respect for one-self and others, and of appreciation of diversity may be taken during early childhood, as children begin to mature and put into place their cognitive and affective frameworks. Discussions about potential values education for young children have centered around several themes, for example:

— respect for self and others, fostering co-operation and conflict resolution skills;

— appreciation of diversity, global awareness and multicultural education;

— practical implementation of the *Convention on the Rights of the Child,* as a set of values universally accepted as essential for children to be able to fulfill their potential;

— the role of pervasive cultural violence, including television, movies, drama portrayals that are stimulated by toys;

— love and respect for nature;

— stimulation of the child's imagination through creativity;

— establishing multi-cultural programmes that help young children integrate spiritual / religious with secular learning, or bridge the gaps of experience often faced by multiple language or multiple cultural groups.

Making the right choice

Declaring that " investment in the development and care of our youngest children is the most fundamental form of good leadership, " Carol Bellamy, UNICEF's Executive Director, argued that the world is squandering human potential on a massive scale as hundreds of millions of the world's youngest citizens flounder in poverty and neglect in their first years of life. Early childhood care is a solid investment. For every $1 spent on early childhood care there is a $7 return through cost savings. This figure is derived from studies showing that participants in pre-school and day care are less likely to suffer illnesses, repeat grades, drop out of school, or require remedial services later in life. Moreover, by shifting money within budgets, nations can create comprehensive programmes for their youngest citizens without adding large sums of money or further depleting their budgets.

Three major challenges loom: poverty, conflict and HIV/AIDS. These three plagues remain the most pressing challenges for the world and compete with early childhood care for funding. In the poorest nations, scarce resources are used to pay loans. By investing in destructive war machines, many countries steal food, clean water, health care and schooling from their citizens. And in some countries, particularly in sub-Saharan Africa, the HIV/AIDS pandemic has stripped health and education budgets to the bone.

"The state of the world's youngest children, citizens with the same rights as all others, is not nearly as good as it should be," Bellamy concluded. "It will only get better when we alter current priorities and accept the sound economic, social and political sense it makes to prioritize the world's youngest."

Programme Guidelines for a Framework for Action on Values Education in Early Childhood

The programme guidelines that follow constitute the foundation for the *Framework's Action Plan,* and are designed to be used by organizations in planning their own values-based early childhood programmes and/or actions.

Goals and objectives

The overall goal of this initiative is to develop a harmonized and common framework to integrate values in early childhood programmes and services by involving different target groups (including policy makers, community leaders, trainers, caregivers, families, parents, children ...).

The main objectives are to:

— suggest guidelines for concrete actions by Member States, educators, families and parents to address the issue of values in early childhood.

— create a value based environment that contributes to the overall physical, socio-emotional and spiritual development of young children.

— create opportunities for institutions and individuals to discuss, learn and come to a better understanding of the ways of introducing, integrating and implementing values in early childhood programmes.

Guiding principles for action

We reaffirm the dignity and worth of every individual,

Believe that Early Childhood Care and Education, in its widest sense, is part of Basic Education and is essential for all children to maximize their learning potential, Agree that a values-based approach to learning and growing-up is fundamental to the nurturing and development of all children, Seek cooperative and practical commitment from all stakeholders to develop the following principles for action:

1. Every child should have the right to early childhood care and education. Early childhood education programmes should be made available to all children.

2. All early childhood programmes should be based on the values of trust and respect, non-discrimination and the right of the child to grow in an environment of peace.

3. The sustainability of quality early childhood programmes should be insured through:

   — creating ownership by educators, parents/care providers and the community.

   — providing quality training of key local people including educators ! building educator-parent/ care provider information systems to create an awareness of children's needs and rights, build preventative skills and disseminate this information widely through radio or television - as appropriate for each country.

   — creating access to quality model programmes that can be easily disseminated.

4. Educators should be trained to create a values-based child-friendly learning environment. Indicators of such an environment include:

   — Adults model values – demonstrating peaceful, respectful and kind methods of communication with children and adults.

   — Interactions with children promote the feelings of being loved, valued, respected, understood and safe.

   — Children are listened to and positive efforts and qualities are acknowledged.

— Educators model tolerance and valuing each and everyone by appreciating differences, diversity and different cultures.

— Rules and limits are clear – there is discipline without anger.

— Mistakes are treated as an opportunity to learn.

5. Children should be educated about values by allowing time and activities to explore values. A values curriculum would include:

— learning a universal values perspective (dignity and respect for each one).

— learning about different values through definitions, discussions, demonstrations and stories.

— understanding different values by engaging in creative play and expressive activities.

— enjoying values through fun activities, songs, dances and movement, feeling the values and nurture the self with the values of peace, love and respect through "quietly being" exercises.

— learning values-based psycho-social skills and practicing these with peers and adults.

6. The family unit should be acknowledged and supported as the heart of the child's life/learning for all of his/her life, through

— providing quality education about parenting to parents and care givers in a values-based learning environment, beginning when possible with the first pregnancy

— engaging parents in exploring their values and how to positively model and nurture values with their children; this could be done in parent groups or through different forms of media.

Key elements

Key elements of a early childhood values-based framework for action should include an appropriate emphasis on :

— integrated policy development where a cooperative climate encourages and supports all stakeholders to come together.

— safeguarded values education from possible political, religious or social abuse. Values education works best when children and human rights are protected.

— ensuring that values education is authentic, experiential and child-centered aiming at incorporating the physical, mental, social and spiritual well being of the child.

— educating and encouraging children to participate in democratic principles, responsible citizenship and involvement in community service - as key principles in values acquisition and internalization.

— promoting dynamic relationships between children and adults through sharing, learning and growing together.

— taking every opportunity for educators to install a dialogue with parents through the child, taking time to observe and to listen, to find solutions and to remain open to suggestions.

Levels of Action and Strategy for a Framework for Action on Values Education in Early Childhood

The following five levels of action were suggested to facilitate the implementation of the Framework for Action:

- *Personal level*: Adults need to learn to express feelings. Children need to learn to listen, model, acknowledge diversity, to have time, to enjoy, to play, feel.
- *Family level*: Parents need to be supported, helped, educated.
- *School level*: Educators need to be trained to take into account emotional and affective attitudes.
- *Community level*: Communities need to have/create places/spaces where children can be welcomed and nurtured, including street children, AIDS children/orphans.
- *State level*: States have the responsibility to implement the Convention on the Rights of the Child and to provide education.

The following process was proposed:

- Undertake immediate individual actions at the local level.
- Start working at the community level by inviting individuals to participate, and then move up through the different levels of action, building networks and alliances to facilitate the work, articulating, teaching, clarifying.
- Get information to support the dissemination of value based actions at district/regional level or joining national efforts (through national teachers associations, health nurses, etc)

— Take into account world summits like the Special Session on Children in September 2001. Cooperate with governments in contributing to reflection for action in a value based framework for Early Childhood Care and Education.

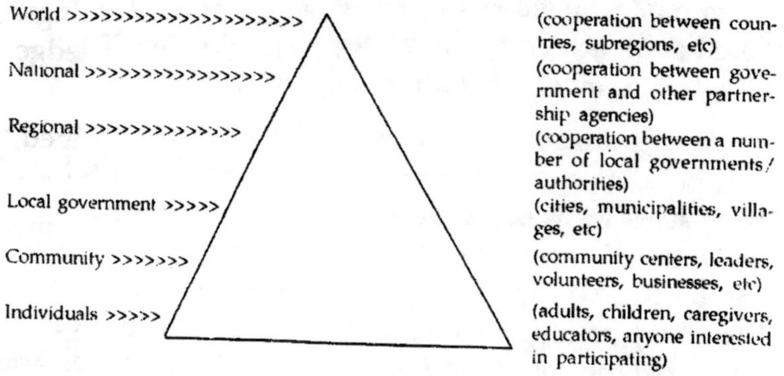

It is important to define a frame of action at every level, in order to create a partnership/network to start working on a joint programme. If we see, at each level, the opportunity to reach young children, through educators (caregivers, kindergarten teachers, nurses, parents, etc ...), and see them as potential role models, we need to give these educators tools and training in values education. This enhanced awareness will help change their approach to themselves and to young children: we need to let children learn to be and learn to live together, but to provide this, we have to live that concept ourselves.

After defining a set of goals and aims, it is necessary to design a clear strategy, since a programme for young children must be multidimensional. It must try to combine different spheres of activities in a common effort to develop integrated services, to move towards an holistic approach, based on the needs of the young children, their parents and their educators, and to arrive at a more comprehensive and multi-faceted programme. Encouraging multi-sectoral collaboration and connecting on-going programmes together can facilitate introducing a values based approach as a natural new way of better living for all who are involved with young children.

Depending on local conditions, different opportunities will help open possibilities of introducing values based approaches for young children with the whole community. For instance, many countries have family health centers run by the Ministry of Health and/or other institutions. Usually, parent groups exist in those centers, and can be easily redesigned to be part of a set of workshops and training sessions for values based parent/family education. Another example are early childhood education programmes (kindergartens, preschools, etc ...) that can start including an introduction to values in daily activities with teachers, assistants, parents and children.

An important asset for moving forward would be the establishment of a Committee for Early Childhood in every community, made of representatives of the early childhood educators, of the parents of young children, of the local community (municipality, neighborhood, etc ..), of the Ministry of Education in the area, of nurses, of paraprofessionals, of NGOs, of the private sector, etc... This Committee, being from different sectors and disciplines, can help plan and implement common work which can lead after a period of time to a more harmonious platform in favour of young children.

Action Plan for a Framework for Action on Values Education in Early Childhood

The *Framework* focuses on seven programme areas for its implementation, each covering a number of actions. Building the Framework requires and depends on joint development, promotion and monitoring. Several implementation mechanisms were suggested for achieving progress in each programme areas. These will be refined and modified as individual organizations map their own mechanisms and strengths.

Seven programme areas

Building the *Framework* requires developing and enhancing the following seven programme areas, which represent different ways we create, build, support and expand the introduction, integration and implementation of value based approaches in early childhood

1.Undertake advocacy/dialogue/awareness raising activities, including.

— Appealing to policy makers through gentle persuasion. They know what is not working. We need to provide clear options.

— Organizing meetings among representatives of different approaches to education.

— Raising consumer awareness on ethics behind products, such as issues of child labor, child exploitation.

— Making use of the networks of UNESCO, UNICEF and Education International for the diffusion and dissemination of information on these topics, in particular in the framework of *the International Decade for a Culture of Peace and Non-Violence for the Children of the World (2001-2010).*

— Increasing educator-parent/care provider information systems by developing user-friendly information briefs on such things as stages of childhood development, values awareness and parenting skills; and writing them in such a way that they could easily be used in or by the media, or in school/nursery newsletters.

— Developing more awareness of children's need for love and protection and children's rights by creating and disseminating such materials.

— Celebrating national/international events with values activities.

— Internet and multimedia

  — create reciprocal web links between organizations represented at this workshop to increase information about resources and good practices.

  — create a website with activities from different programmes, resources and links, and serve as a depository for values stories from and for different cultures.

  — expand the Living Values Education Program web site's "Children Participate" section, so that children can share what they are doing in their exploration about values from any programmes.

2. Develop and offer training, including

— Providing quality training of key local people including educators, parents and business people to insure sustainability of quality early childhood programmes. This could include the following elements:

— Create a personalized sense of the importance of a values-based child-centered approach and a sense of ownership by leading key stakeholders in a values awareness session in which they generate elements of a values-based atmosphere and offer their perception of children's needs.

— Continue to involve local leaders in sessions in which they generate ideas for and cooperate in creating healthy community resources for children and families.

— Build awareness in the community about the importance of children's needs and rights and the wisdom and efficacy of a nurturing and preventative approach through the media.

— Training local educators to understand and use model quality child-centered, values-based education programmes. This would include the following elements:

  — Include some local educators who are professionals and have the ability to train other local teachers, train parent group leaders, and interact with the local community.

  — Train in such a way that the educators experience the kind of atmosphere they are to provide to the children, i.e. focus not just on content but on the process.

— Encourage them to add elements from their own heritage and the cultures in the area.

— Develop model sites where other people working with children from 0 to 8 can observe.

3. Enhance prevention and protection, including

— Creating a safe environment for children. This is based on the statistics that injury is the first cause of morbidity and mortality in children aged 0 to 17 - in particular for young children between the ages of 0 and 4. The amazing fact is that 95% of these injuries can be prevented, by education and safe environments.

— Providing all formal institutions for children (such as daycare centers, family health care centers, clinics, kindergartens, schools, etc.) with safety devices.

— Supporting/developing, on a national level, programmes for promoting safety in the environment of children (homes, backyards, streets, etc.). It should include educational programmes for parents (and of course educators, health workers, etc.), advertizing in the media, and reducing the prices of safety devices used in homes, backyards and cars, bicycles.

4. Create supports and advocacy through media and communications, including

— Creating an awareness among media people that consciously or unconsciously they convey "not so friendly" values to young children - it seems that there is reporting about young children in case of abuse or violent death but rarely on more "normal" daily life.

— Encouraging value based media messages for children. "Packaging" the principles of action or concrete recommendations for value based early childhood programmes so that they can be readily use by media professionals.

— Making sure the *Children's Television Charter* is widely known and implemented. The Charter stresses the right of children to receive quality programmes, and the right to see and express themselves, their culture, their language and life experiences through media.

— Exploring the needs of young audiences and promoting a variety of initiatives, vital to securing the right of all children to quality media.

— Exploring the effects of globalization on children's audiovisual media, and requiring regulation that prevents violent programmes during children's viewing time.

— Encouraging the creation of national TV channels and/or programmes on parenting and child rearing, providing experiences from educators, parents, etc.

5. *Mobilize and involve business/private sector, including*

— Identifying possibilities of using the *Global Compact* (with the business community launched by the UN Secretary-General) for the establishment of partnerships with the private sector in the area of early childhood and values education.

— Encouraging businesses to supply early childhood programmes for employees by employing early childhood educators. A Montessori educator, for example, could teach children in the morning and provide advice to adults and train local parents on early childhood related topics in the afternoon.

— Encouraging the private sector to be involved in initiatives to fight social exclusion and poverty.

— Creating an awareness among businesses of the incentives to invest in early childhood development efforts. In particular, early childhood initiatives:

  — enable companies to compete for, and retain, the best workers. Employees who have access to family support policies are more likely to remain on the job and show more initiative than workers with no access to these policies.

  — increase productivity and reduce employee turnover and absenteeism.

  — invest in the building of a highly-educated, productive workforce in the future. By making sure that children receive good quality care in the earliest years, businesses can help build a productive workforce for the future.

6. Identify, utilize and build upon networks, partnerships and affinity groups, including

— Establishing partnerships for children, encouraging participation of every individual in the society at different levels: parents, families, teachers, nurses, politicians, educators to joint efforts for the best development of the child.

— Sharing of perspectives and mutual learning to build upon the concept of partnership and complementarity.

— Working in cooperation with affinity groups to achieve outreach, impact, consensus, and common cause with related issues: children's rights, women, environment, etc.

— Developing issue-specific and action-oriented partnerships so as to piggyback issues on related movements and to tie early childhood concerns to current public problems.

7. Assess effectiveness and monitor progress, including

— Calling for the concerned and committed attention of professionals working in collaboration with programme providers and participants to conduct proper programme evaluation.

— Evaluating regularly the programme using criteria that consider the overall contributions and relevance of the programme to every child and the society; this includes comprehensive and continuous evaluation in terms of the programme's attainment of local, regional, national and international standards for excellence in the care and education of young children.

— Adopting a cycle of Reflective Self Monitoring and Assessment practices, e.g. plan, do, review, befitting the ethos and commitment of the school.

— Using quality based values learning indicators.

— Selecting a small number of indicators at a time (3 for instance) - one for planning, one for doing, one for reviewing - time managed and designed to fit one's own needs.

— Establishing processes for determining community expectations and guidelines for quality programmes and services, for community-based dialogue and debate about how the needs of children are addressed.

Next Steps: Towards Implementation of Child Friendly Learning Environments

There is nothing stopping us from making a difference to all children's learning.

Together we can help children to know, to do, to be, to belong and to give love. Together we can help children to be themselves, know themselves, make sense of their own world, make sense of the world around them, serve others and be stewards of their own environment.

The *Framework* will be widely disseminated for comments, additions and support. The *Framework* will be placed under the umbrella of the International Decade for a Culture of Peace and *Non-Violence for the Children of the World*, which offers a good frame of reference for any work related to children and values.

Several possible "commitments" were suggested: (with the understanding that each organization must in fact define its own participation in this joint initiative):

— participate in an email/fax/postal discussion on Early Childhood and Values Education;

— take part in the mapping / resource / information sharing exercise to compile a *Book of Guidelines*, including providing information to put on Internet;

— find ways in which your organization can contribute to the regional process and to share information on this initiative with the largest possible audience;

— look at ways your organization can/does contribute financially to the process of fostering better values based early childhood initiatives;

— getting others to contribute and participate in this initiative.

Identify ways to contribute to the Framework and invite others to participate:

It is up to each organization to determine its own goals, resources, and interest in this joint process. As organizations identify ways they can contribute, these will be pieced together by UNESCO and LVEP, who can look for ways to coordinate/facilitate sharing and collaboration at regional and international levels. Regional meetings will be convened to initiate information and knowledge exchange on the issue of values and young children.

Several suggestions and possible offers were made to further the discussions held during the *International Workshop* and involve other organizations and various subregions, these will have to be explored in the coming months. These meetings will help reach out to other organizations who have not been part of this mechanism, inviting them to participate and contribute, and informing them of evolution within this shared Framework. UNESCO will launch and promote the Framework as a mobilization tool for values-based early childhood in its Member States.

Compile a Book of Guidelines

In order to illustrate how values can be integrated into early childhood programmes/services, a two-part sourcebook will be designed and compiled showing diverse experiences and what makes them work in different communities, regions, countries. This will be done through contacting colleagues and partners around the globe working in a variety of contexts and cultures to share user friendly evidence on using values in early childhood. A part of the sourcebook would show, step by step, clearly and in simple terms, a range of ways towards starting and implementing values education for young children in different contexts and with a variety of partners. Thus someone eager to embark on such a programme without knowing how to go about it, would become acquainted with the basic notions required to take action. The other part of the sourcebook would illustrate these step by step approaches by telling success stories of experiences carried out in a number of communities and countries.

Develop training materials/modules for young children at risk

In response to the growing number of young children at risk, of younger children affected by the spread of AIDS but also the increasing number of younger street children, Living Values, in cooperation with UNESCO and other partners, will design during 2001 some draft materials/ modules to use with young street children and those who work with them, and also for working with young children affected by AIDS.

2

Innovative Schools Practices

The term 'at risk' is generally used to describe young people considered vulnerable to, and affected by a range of factors likely to impede their successful transition to a fulfilling adult life. Within an educational context, the notion of being 'at risk' specifically refers to those young people considered unlikely to complete school to Year 12 and therefore tends to relate to initiatives directed at increasing school retention rates.

Whilst childhood is often marked out as a time of vulnerability and risk taking, some children are exposed to far greater levels of life-factors that place them at risk' A useful way of conceptualising the notion of 'at risk' is proposed by McWhirter et al., who view risk on a continuum. At the 'minimal risk' end of the continuum are young people who have at their disposal a range of factors to protect them from risk, such as positive experiences within the family, school and society and limited environmental stressors.

The continuum moves through 'remote risk ', high risk' and 'imminent risk' ending with the group of young people who are 'at risk' and actively engaging in dangerous behaviours and experiencing extreme vulnerability. Young people will fall onto this continuum of risk at different points, based on the degree to which their behaviour or situation increases the likelihood of further marginalising them or increasing their vulnerability.

According to Withers and Russell, those at the more extreme points on the at risk continuum are more likely to experience multiple 'negative future events' (such as educational under-achievement, early school leaving, drug abuse, delinquency, offending and criminal behaviour, suicide) which decrease their chances of developing and sustaining satisfying, fulfilling and responsible lives. Along this continuum, Fuller describes an alternative model for viewing risk behaviour, in which risk is conceptualised as a feature of developmental trajectories through adolescence. According to Fuller there are six trajectories, including:

— Stable adaptive functioning;

— Stable maladaptive functioning;

— Adolescent turn around or recovery;

— Adolescent decline;

— Mid adolescent dip; and

— Puberty troubles.

Viewing risk on a continuum or within developmental trajectories highlights the cumulative and circular nature of risk and the need to understand young people and school participation within an holistic framework beyond single-issue identification. Early identification of vulnerable young people is seen as an essential first line of defense against the negative outcomes at the more extreme end of the continuum. However, some argue that caution needs to be taken to ensure that early identification does not become a self-fulfilling indicator of negative outcomes through singling out or 'labelling' young people who are seen to be deviating from an acceptable norm.

Batten and Russell developed a widely reported summary and classification of 'at risk' factors, However, the definition of 'students at risk' employed by Batten and Russell does not refer just to the risk of premature school leaving, but to the more fundamental risk of educational under-achievement and more broadly still to those young people beset by particular difficulties and disadvantages who are thought likely to fail to achieve the development in their adolescent years that would provide a sound basis for a satisfying and fulfilling adult life. It should not be assumed that all the specific factors necessarily relate to the risk of early school leaving.

Risk factors are usefully grouped into those relating to attributes of the individual, the family, the school and to broader societal circumstances. Table 1 shows the diversity of attributes or circumstances that impinge on young people's chances of benefiting fully from school, and of achieving to the best of their ability.

Table 1 Risk Factors

The Individual

Psychological factors

- Low self esteem
- Low motivation
- Primitive cognitive constructs, faulty beliefs
- Low intelligence
- Inability to relate
- Poor bonding to family, school

- High level of aggression

Physical factors

- Poor health, illness & disability
- Low birth weight
- Low level of autonomic & central nervous system arousal

Behavioural

- Disruptive behaviour
- Hyperactivity
- Passivity
- Early pregnancy/ motherhood
- Offending
- Substance use/abuse
- Poor academic performance
- Early, chronic truancy
- Association with antisocial peers, adults
- Sex work
- Social isolation

The Family

Family structure

- Fragmented, reconstituted family structures
- Large family size
- Separation from family

Family functioning

- Poor family management practices
- Disturbed parent-child relationships
- Conflict
- Abuse
- Modelling on antisocial parents
- High mobility
- Family disorganisation

Family socioeconomic status

- Low parental income
- Low parental education attainment
- Unemployment

School Factors

School organisation

- Rigid organisational policies
- Repressive discipline
- No help for early leavers & barriers to re-entry
- Large class size
- Large school without substructures

Curriculum

- Unstimulating content
- No participation in decision-making
- Passive teaching learning strategies
- Competitive exam dominated assessment

School climate

- Unsupportive school culture
- Negative teacher/ student relationships
- Negative peer relationships
- Absence of school counsellors
- Lack of student participation
- Poor school/ home relationships
- Poor staff professional development

Community and Social Factors

- Extreme poverty
- Anti-social community norms
- Neighbourhood disorganisation
- Demographic factors: males and non-anglo ethnic groups

Identification of risk factors is only useful if it helps explain the processes or forces that lead to disengagement with school and then guides how these processes can be intercepted to ensure young people are assisted to get the most from educational opportunities. Commenting on the nature of the relationship between risk factors and negative educational outcomes, Batten and Russell note:

— Cause-effect relationships between single risk factors and educational outcomes should be ruled out as overly simplistic as should many of the models positing intervening variables.

— Relationships need instead to be viewed as forming a dense and complex web of interrelated, interacting, multi-directional forces.

Lastly, a public discourse about risk factors runs the risk of labelling schools as schools for 'at risk' students or 'welfare' schools, with the effect that parents may send their children to other schools. There is potentially a major disincentive for schools to develop programmes and initiatives to retain at risk young people who would otherwise leave.

Types of School Leavers

Researches during the late '80s and early '90s produced a typology of school leavers structured around young people's perceptions of school and the external circumstances that might detach them from the education system. A later version of this typology is given below.

— *Positive leavers*: Those who leave early to take up employment, an apprenticeship or some alternative career path; in general a positive choice for the young person.

  Response: Referral assistance or advice about training schemes etc may be needed, but these young people are less likely to be at risk than other early leavers.

— *Opportune leavers*: These 'leavers' take the opportunity to leave in the hope that they may get employment even though they have generally not settled on a definite 'career path'.

Response: In the short-term, this group may not be interested in referral or advice; in the medium to long term, they may respond favourably to a 'second chance' or re-entry training programme.

— *Would be leavers*: The 'reluctant stayers', who lack opportunities beyond school and so remain.

  Response: Evidence on curriculum innovation does suggest that with opportunity for better teacher/student relationships, and student participation and negotiation over curriculum content, these students may find school more satisfying.

— *Circumstantial leavers*: These are young people forced out of school for non educational reasons: children from low income families and those with change family income support circumstances are particularly vulnerable here.

  Response: While curriculum innovation may help these students' level of satisfaction with school, it may not improve their retention. Changes to income support provisions could be a crucial factor; schools should also consider a more flexible policy on attendance, allowing for those who either need the income from a part-time job or whose level of interest would benefit from greater flexibility.

— *Discouraged leavers*: Those who have not experienced success in their schooling and whose level of performance and interest in school is low.

  Response: More flexible school policies and curriculum choices may help to reduce the numbers of these leavers whose experience of education has been a discouraging one. Special programs need to be devised which cater for a diversity of learning styles. Pastoral support mechanisms may also be important.

— *Alienated leavers*: Similar to discouraged leavers, but are identified as having greater needs and would possibly be more difficult to re-engage.

  Response: More flexible school policies with regard to curriculum organisation and attendance requirements could reduce the level and extent of alienation, but the postschool experiences of this group are likely to be far more crucial. This raises issues about alternative programs and services provided at a local or community level to re-engage these leavers within a non-school context.

This typology highlights the intermediary role of schools in activating or enabling the risk for some young people. For example, students who become homeless may 'drift' out of schools uncommitted to meeting their special support needs or they may be 'driven out' of schools following poor attendance and performance resulting from their homelessness.

Chamberlain and MacKenzie have documented the contingent 'career' process that may happen for a young person who becomes homeless, leading to serious hazards to their health and well-being and ultimately for some, long-term or chronic homelessness. Similar career scenarios can be envisaged for other issues such as substance abuse and criminal offending. Thus the goals of increased school retention and improved educational attainment, can be effective in reducing harm and improving employment prospects.

Reasons for Leaving Schools

Young people dislike, disengage from, or leave school for a variety of reasons, at different stages of their schooling, with different attitudes towards education and different prospects for future careers. Thus there cannot be a single dominant 'typical' description of the early school-leaving group. In their study of school leavers in three areas in Victoria, Melton, St. Kilda and Shepparton, Holden and Dwyer noted that many of the 132 leavers 'drifted' out of school rather than making a conscious decision. The two most common reasons given by young people for leaving school (over 20 per cent in both cases) were first, finding school boring and second, negative experience with teachers. These young people were considerably more likely to leave because of a negative experience of school rather than a positive sense of what existed outside school (just over five per cent left school to take up a specific job). Girls were more likely than boys to report difficulties with family and health issues and school, but less likely than boys to actually leave school early.

The three most prevalent explanations for leaving prior to Year 12 emerging from the Australian Institute of Family Studies survey of 15-19 year olds in Victoria were: desire to start earning, lack of interest in further schooling, and poor academic performance. Of these, lack of interest was the most frequently cited reason by both young people (75 per cent) and their parents (78 per cent). Low motivation to finish Year 12 is seen by the authors as a failure on the part of schools to address the curriculum and other needs of all their students. The Australian findings on young people's reasons for leaving school are broadly similar to the results from international studies of school leavers and at-risk young people.

Effects of School Culture

If there is one consistent theme that cuts across all the complexity and diversity associated with early school leaving it is that the school culture ultimately is what makes the difference. Holden and Dwyer identified the following problems:

— A non-stimulating environment that has no discernible relation to the wider community or the adult world to which the young person is beginning to gain access;

— Lack of support and referral to appropriate agencies for young people who are experiencing problems in their personal and academic lives; and

— Negative teacher/student relationships which are propped up by rules and regulations which disallow young people from expressing themselves as adult and responsible members of the school community.

Students don't drop out of school because they do not want to learn. They drop out because they are failing to learn. Everyone wants to learn if the outcome serves a purpose and the process is more positive than negative.

On the basis of an extensive literature review, Bradley isolated nine areas of school life that were important influences on students' decisions about staying or leaving. These factors are summarised below:

— *Curriculum*: More practical, job-oriented subjects; more life skills and personal development orientation; more choice, less compulsion, fewer prerequisites; altered duration; more sporting and recreational subjects.

- *Teaching-Learning Process:* More independent and individualised work; more student-centred work; more tutorial assistance; more hands-on, activity-based, experiential learning experiences; more class discussions; less homework; more excursions and camps.
- *Assessment and Credentials*: Fewer exams; more progressive assessment; more feedback; more criterion-referenced assessment; more transfer of credit from institutions; less competition; higher status to those who graduate from secondary school; more broadly defined university entrance requirements.
- *Relationships and Climate:* More caring and supportive; more friendly, relaxed and informal; more counselling and guidance; more pastoral assistance; more opportunities for students and teachers to socialise; mentoring programs.
- *Discipline and Control:* Fewer/different rules; more democracy; more student representation; more freedom for students; stricter/more lenient enforcement; tighter record-keeping.
- *School Organisation&Administration:* Smaller school and class sizes; divisions into 'mini-schools.; separate school/campus for senior students; altered length or timing of the school day; more flexible timetable; vertical grouping of students; more options for part-time study and return-to-study.
- *Environment and resources*: Improved buildings and grounds; improved teaching spaces and resources; improved sporting and recreational facilities and equipment.

Dwyer et al provided a useful framework for thinking about young people's reasons for staying at/leaving school.

- When young people are asked why they stay at school they tend to give very general answers about the value of education or else highly specific, instrumental reasons. Five types of reason for staying are apparent:
  - A general understanding that staying at school is what one does.
  - A success in learning and its associated pleasure/ joy/ acceptance.
  - Pressure of or from families (social, economic, comparative).
  - The importance of social links (friends at school).
- Young people talk about why they left school both in terms of a breakdown in the positive reasons for education:
  - The collapse of a tradition of going to school.
  - Not being able to see that future outcomes exist.
  - A lack of success in learning.
  - The lack of family pressure or value on education.
  - The lack of social links (no friends, friends elsewhere, etc).
- As a growth in the negative impact of school (school is an actively unpleasant experience):
  - Social failure: lack of friends etc through bullying.

— Outcome (learning) failure: not succeeding at school, not understanding, not getting anywhere.

— Personal (behavioural) failure: being in trouble, resisting, being put down.

In contrast with the positive alternatives perceived to exist outside school:

— *Social success*: friends located out of school, with time etc (socially nicer/ more exciting places to hang out).

— *Outcome (earning) success*: possibilities of immediate income (income support, legitimate earning or black economy).

— *Personal (behavioural) success*: possibilities for roles of value and esteem.

Barriers to Returning

Dwyer et al's push/pull model of early school leaving also applies to would-be returnees. This [negative] attitude not only precludes them from the secondary education system - they tend to transfer it to anything that has the slightest connotation of learning and thus tends to keep the young people from undertaking any further education and, to some extent, training programs

Some of the young people interviewed by Holden wanted to return to secondary school, but were refused entry because of their past behaviour and perceptions of their being troublemakers. The 28 young people who did return tended to explain their choice in terms of trying to get the minimum standard of education that would enable them to find work. Although generally committed to learning, the majority left again before completing Year 12. The main problems these young people encountered on returning to school were:

— Late re-enrolments which mean they were unable to study their preferred subjects.

— Negative reaction from school staff who tended to offer little encouragement or support to young people returning to their old school.

— Lack of general support within the school because of a tendency to ignore or underplay the difficulties faced by young people returning to school.

— Lack of adequate financial support.

— Placement in classes with younger people who were not as committed to learning.

— Troublesome classroom and schoolyard dynamics associated with the age discrepancies between the young people who are returning and the other students.

— Having to return to an environment that allows individuals the minimum of autonomy and responsibility.

— Finding school and the curriculum even less relevant to them once they had made the attempt to establish themselves as independent adults.

Startegies of Intervention

Recognition of the diversity of experiences and reasons that lead young people to leave school early, highlights the need for a range of approaches and a consequent need to *match* young people with appropriate responses. Dwyer et al, suggested three essential components of an education-focused response:

— The development of core social and relational skills.

— The development of roles of real value for young people.

— The development of appropriate and targeted skills.

School under-achievement, failure and drop out have been attributed to a range of factors including: the cognitive abilities, motivation and personality of an individual; peer acceptance and influence; family practices and relationships; community attitudes and support for learning, and community economic status; and the characteristics of the school setting, including structure, curriculum, student-teacher relationships and peer interactions.

Poverty is one of the greatest risk factors associated with problem behaviours, including those described above, and delinquency, crime and violence. Low economic status communities are often characterised by a lack of social and personal supports or resources, including health care, child care, housing, education, job training, employment and recreation.

Protective Factors

Resilience is a term used for a range of protective factors that have effects in the opposite direction to risk factors. Protective factors, or resilience will help a young person remain at school and cope with the pressures and problems that might otherwise lead them to leave school early. Protective factors may be contextual or external to the individual—in their school or community environment - or on the other hand, internal characteristics of the individual.

While external risk factors contribute significantly to participation in risk behaviours, not all young people will succumb to the extreme end of the scale. Shifting the balance from vulnerability to resilience requires decreasing exposure to those risk factors, or increasing the availability of protective factors. Factors contributing to resilience in young people include personal factors such as social competence, problem solving, autonomy and sense of purpose, as well as family connectedness and positive relationships, and peer and adult support beyond the home.

The existence of protective factors is believed to reduce the impact of risks, or change the way a person responds to these risks, thus shielding them from negative outcomes.

Fuller describes the four main factors promoting well-being in students as: peer connectedness; fitting in at school; feeling loved by your family to the extent that they help you to understand yourself better; and having an adult outside your family take a positive interest in you. Again, the concept of connectedness, of belonging to a family, an area, a friendship group or school, is seen as crucial to building resilience in young people.

Several researchers have pointed to the importance of protective factors that make young people more resilient, that is, less susceptible to risk. The protective factors identified in the international literature are identified by Withers and Russell are given below:

— *Individual Characteristics*: Resilient temperament, positive social orientation; high intelligence; ability to think abstractly and critically, to foresee consequences and to appreciate the feelings of victims; high selfesteem; social competence, problem-solving skills, autonomy and sense of purpose.

— *School:* Reinforced participation/involvement in school and belief in its values; bonding to school; school connectedness - feeling that teachers treat students fairly, feeling part of school and close to people there; availability of counselling from teachers; caring and supportive teachers; high expectations, including emphasis on learning progress, clearly stated rules and student involvement in activities; opportunities to participate and be responsible.

— *Peer Group:* Reinforced activity/ involvement with pro-social peers and belief in their values; bonding to pro-social peers.

— *Family:* Cohesion; reinforced activity or involvement in pro-social family and belief in their values; warmth or bonding during childhood; emotional 'coaching' of the child by parents; connectedness to parents in mutually close, caring relationship and emotional support from wider family or trusted others; closeness to one person, with affection expressed physically and verbally; clear, prosocial family norms and rules; high expectations.

— *Community*: External social supports that reinforce the individual's competencies and commitments and provide a belief system; caring and support through availability of community resources; reinforced activity/ involvement with pro-social community members and belief in their values; high expectations and opportunities for participation; perceived importance of religion and prayer; availability of counselling from church.

Intervention Principles

While emphasising that not all young people face the same degree of risk, all young people are vulnerable to some extent. The difficulty of identifying risk and the fact that the young people themselves as well as their circumstances change over time means that intervention should not be geared only for those at the high risk end of the spectrum. It should take into account the needs of all young people in modern society where the value and meaning of education is changing. At the same time, it is noted that not all young people who face risk 'succumb' by engaging in anti-social behaviours or behaviours that compromise their health and future prospects.

Withers and Russell developed a list of twenty intervention principles and a preferred model of intervention that offers an holistic approach to provision, encompassing both prevention and intervention. Withers and Russell suggested a full service schools approach, but in its detail somewhat different from the full service school advocated by Dryfoos:

The full service school is conceived of as one in which high quality education and a range of support services are offered in a comprehensive, collaborative, non-fragmented way, so that the educational, physical, psychological and social requirements of students and families are met rationally and holistically. A 'full service approach' to addressing early school leaving has two prongs: first, schools and education systems require some significant structural reform to more adequately support at risk students as a mainstream commitment; and second, the need to help young people and their families by providing health and other social support services on school sites or linked to schools.

Dwyer details some of the changes schools will have to make to enable effective strategies and just as importantly, some of the necessary changes at the system level that will in turn enable schools to realise the potential of early leaving prevention.

Role of the School

Over the past decade there has been a number of initiatives directly funded by both Commonwealth and State/Territory governments with the aim of increasing school participation. While a school's culture is a key variable in determining the extent of early school leaving, it is also clear that many factors outside the school make full participation in education very difficult for some young people. Strategies aimed at enabling young people to continue their education must of course extend beyond the school and into the wider range of services and supports—just how far beyond is still the subject of debate.

There is a movement in the USA to restructure and/or reorient the focus of schools. This movement is based on the suggestion that while at risk students may have more complex needs or more issues than the average student, in any student population there will be many students who have some problem(s) at some time during their schooling. There is a growing body of argument that broadens the description of what makes an 'effective., 'good' or exemplary school in the 21st Century. Within the debate is a whole range of suggested strategies from variations on the theme of full service schools to basic attempts to ensure schools at least have access to a school welfare co-ordinator.

The potential of the school is by now well recognised. Particularly, the school is the site where early identification of problems can be attempted, tracking risk circumstances undertaken, and an unthreatening first point of contact for a range of community-wide supports and services provided.

'The school provides an excellent locus for the provision of holistic,integrated and collaborative services, given the central part the schoolplays in the life of the child and young person over an extended period of *time*'.

Some of the characteristics of schools which are effective in dealing with the needs and concerns of at risk young people have been identified by Druin & Butler as including:

— Strong leadership.

— High levels of commitment from staff.

— School climate.

— Individualised curriculum.

— Orientation to work and learning in the classroom.

Wardman and Kimclaimed that proposals to 'fix' the education system through a focus on individual 'bits and pieces' such as changes in curriculum, voucher systems and teacher training will not deliver long term sustainable change. Rather, they propose a fundamental shift in thinking about the purpose and value of education, and how the educational system should fit into the rest of society.

In the literature on resilience there are claims that teachers have the power to 'tip the scale from risk to resilience' through caring relationships, positive and high expectations and the provision of opportunities to participate and contribute. The implication to be drawn is that change will require not only the proliferation of new practices of student support, but also whole of school change will have to be backed up and mandated by systemic guidelines, policies and appropriate resource allocations.

Barriers preventing teachers and schools achieving the best for students are usually associated with students not having a strong connection to the school. This lack of connection may result from inflexible curriculum pathways, lack of relevance of teaching and learning programs, a poor value being attached to education by parents or caregivers, inadequate skill or confidence levels of teachers, feeling unsafe in the school environment, poor social connectedness or an inability to participate in a valued way in the classroom and life of the school.

Models of School-based Intervention

Brooks et al., in an Autstralian National Youth Affairs Research Scheme (NYARS) report on *Under-age school leaving*, presented an overview of 34 initiatives at Commonwealth and State/Territory level which addressed under-age or early school leaving specifically or as part of a broader strategy for student support. The focus of their empirical investigation was on the specific initiatives that had evolved within schools and/or communities in response to under-age school leaving. They highlighted the diversity of initiatives, both in objectives and strategies.

In spite of this diversity, the 34 initiatives could be classified as operating predominantly in terms of one of six intervention models. This typology is structured on the basis of where specific activities or engagement occur (school/outside school) and the breadth of the program in the school itself (targeted/universal). They described the structures employed by initiatives to provide support and assistance to 'potential under-age school leavers':

— *Community-based partial withdrawal:* students are withdrawn from mainstream school on a part-time or temporary basis to a project operating in a community setting, with the aim of eventually reintegrating students back into mainstream schools.

— *School-based partial withdrawal:* students are withdrawn from normal classes to participate in an alternative programme operating within the school. The initiative may operate as a full-time or part-time annexe within a school or as a 'time-out' programme where students participate in individual or small-group sessions that run parallel to normal classes.

— *Community school*: comprehensive education and support program operating as an alternative to mainstream school. Participants are usually not expected to return to mainstream school.

— *Outreach services:* provision of specialist support services to a number of schools within a particular geographic area. Administration is usually located off-campus, with staff travelling to schools to deliver services.

— *Integrated whole school:* characterised by a generalist focus on the needs of potential under-age school leavers across the whole school rather than specific initiatives which only target at risk students. The emphasis is on innovations or enhancements to student education and welfare support measures which are undertaken within normal school processes.

— *Event-based:* focus on one particular activity, such as wilderness excursion or cultural camp. This approach aims to provide an intensive experience to help 'turn young people around.

Withers and Russell also devised a typology of school-based modules which they grouped into types of programme design, varying according to: stage in school trajectory (pre-primary, primary, middle years and so on); degree of risk (through low risk to moderate and high risk); extent to which initiative is mainstream or targeted.

Their categories resolved into six main groups:

— *Full service modules*: seeing young person as a whole and offering that person a service which is holistic rather than fragmented, with the school as site of those integrated services.

— Years before schooling modules.

— Early primary years modules.

— *Middle-school modules*: have special pertinence to Years 5-9 and may have broader applicability.

— *Moderate risk student modules*: designs for special institutions or programs intended for intensive interventions on behalf of moderate risk students away from the sites of mainstream schooling.

— High risk student modules: away from sites of mainstream schooling.

The Brooks classification focused mainly on levels of intervention and the factors that favour interventions at a particular level. On the other hand, Withers and Russell focused more on the criteria for the appropriateness of a particular intervention—i.e., whether an intervention was designed for early primary students or middle school students, or high risk as opposed to moderate risk students. Both are useful, but have been designed with different purposes in mind.

More recently other initiatives and approaches have been developed to support individual students, such as mentoring and peer support. Case management has also become a key strategy in many schools. In addition, there is an increasing number of innovative approaches to curriculum design such as project based learning, work preparation and work experience.

Effectiveness of Strategies

Withers and Batten undertook a survey of literature on the diversity in programme approaches and objectives from USA, UK and Canada, drew up a list of 13 recurring features of effective programmes that result in real achievement by young people.

The 13 features are:

— attention to the whole person, incorporating social and personal as well as academic and vocational development;

— a focus on practical learning, related to the student's life experiences and linked, where appropriate, to a vocational pathway;

— encouragement of students to take responsibility for their own learning and behaviour, and to be involved in decisions about the learning process, including the use of incentives and negotiated contracts;

— providing students with the opportunity to work cooperatively with others, both inside and outside the classroom;

— high expectations of students, and provision of programs which challenge and extend;

— positive reinforcement of achievement, building on student strengths;

— establishment of a caring, supportive environment;

— organisational and operational flexibility in order to be able to respond to individual needs;

— concern for students at risk that extends beyond the program through the use of follow-up contact and monitoring;

— appropriate evaluation of student progress by the use of assessment that matches the learning that has taken place; and evaluation of the effectiveness of programs;

— careful selection of program teachers and leaders, and the provision of professional development opportunities for people in those roles;

— integration of school-based programs for students as risk into mainstream educational provision;

— involvement of parents and community in a collaborative endeavour for young people at risk, and a fostering of links with agencies outside the school.

When thinking about appropriate measures of success, a distinction should be made between those initiatives aiming at across-the-board 'dropout prevention' and those targeting moderate and high risk groups. A common experience of initiatives attempting the latter has been to reconsider an exclusive focus on short-term educational outcomes.

Innovation and Best Practice

The UNESCO International Commission on Education for the Twenty-first Century identified the major shifts and changes in societies around the world in the past few decades and the need for education to face up to this problem now more than ever as a world society struggles painfully to be born: education is at the heart of both personal and community development; its mission is to enable each of us, without exception, to develop our creative potential, including responsibility for our own lives and achievement of our personal aims.

The goal of reducing early school leaving has led to changes in the way schools operate. Since 1995 in particular, considerable effort has gone into initiatives to encourage and resource projects and programs to assist at risk students and reduce early school leaving.

'Best practice', in the context of assisting at risk young people, means identifying sound directions and promising, effective strategies and initiatives. Best Practice is much more than this. It is practice widely recognised as standing out in a field and, when replicated, it produces consistent results at the highest level of effectiveness. It also means identifying the initiatives that have been successful both for individuals and systems change, and developing standards and/or benchmarks for future action and measurement.

Innovation and best practice strategies will have differing impacts on the school involved. For example, the introduction of a tutoring or mentoring program may have very little impact on the rest of the school, whereas the development of a whole-of-school approach will require major rethinking of the school culture, teacher attitudes and community relationships.

Educational and Community Change

With most current organisational forms and processes facing major shifts and changes, management theory and practice is grappling with the need for new approaches to organisations. Much of this debate is applicable to educational organisations, given the major and complex changes happening both in the broader community and the schooling system. Some of the relevant concepts include 'school improvement', new visions and outcomes, schools as learning organisations as well as 'quality management., 'best practice' and 'school effectiveness'.

Huberman and Miles undertook a major study of school improvement concentrating on the process of innovation. They identified a number of generic or basic dilemmas likely to be faced in any process of implementing innovation in schools. These were:

— *Fidelity versus Adaptation*: the extent to which models should be adopted and implemented according to conceptual plan or modified and adapted to local constraints and circumstances.

— *Centralised versus Dispersed Influence*: the extent to which central policies and expectations or guidelines should guide an innovation.

— *Co-ordination versus Flexibility*: how much flexibility is helpful given that too much can disperse the impact of an innovation.

— *Ambition versus Practicality*: the pragmatic and practical compromises that may be needed to implement an idea.

The UNESCO Commission identified a number of tensions which are central to the problems of education in the twenty-first century:

— The tension between global and local.

— The tension between the universal and the individual.

— The tension between tradition and modernity.

— The tension between long-term and short-term considerations.

— The tension between the need for competition and equality of opportunity.

— The tension between the expansion of knowledge and human being's capacity to assimilate it.

— The tension between the spiritual and material.

The UNESCO Commission stressed the need for a long-term approach to reform and change, while not underestimating the need to carefully manage short-term problems. They noted that too many short-term changes can be the death of longer-term reform as 'many reformers adopt an approach that is either too radical or too theoretical, ignoring what can be usefully learned from experience or rejecting past achievements.

Much of the change management and innovation literature focuses on a particular innovation and examines the complexities of the processes whereby that innovation is disseminated and adopted.

The precepts offered by the seminal study by Huberman and Miles discuss school change in relation to a fairly narrowly defined set of innovative changes. The multiplicity of particular innovations that come into play under the agenda of supporting at risk students adds a new dimension of complexity to an already complex process.

Organisations are constantly changing, whether to adapt to new external conditions or because the process of internal development moves them through distinct phases and types of structure.

The UNESCO Commission acknowledged the need for teachers and parents to play a major role in bringing about their reform agenda while at the same time requiring *policy makers to face* up squarely to their responsibilities. They cannot leave it to market forces or to some kind of self-regulation to put things right.

Offering a more managerial model for the process, Roger Plant views bringing about change in an organisation also as a five-stage process:

1. Acknowledging the need to change.
2. Mobilising commitment within the organisation.
3. Building a shared vision.
4. Discerning current reality.

5. Making it happen.

In managing change, some of the most common barriers include:

— Same word, different meanings.

— Differing views about what works.

— Accountability and measurement.

— Competition and power.

— Decision making.

— Leadership.

Much of current management literature highlights the key measure of successful management in the 1990s and beyond as the capacity to seize the opportunities presented by organisational change and to lead and drive that change. Organisational change is the key to improving the quality of service delivery and internal management of the organisation.

The experience in Canada Education Research Information System of bringing about change, designed to implement learnings from effective schools projects, found the following factors influenced educational change:

— Fundamental aspects of school culture influence the planning process.

— Leadership is crucial to change.

— Staff changing schools can negatively effect change.

— The central office plays an important role in change within schools.

— The key strategy for change is staff development.

— Ad hoc committees and pilot projects support change effectively.

— Change processes must be able to integrate multiple innovations.

— Goals should be set first at the school level, then at the classroom level.

In creating an effective or best practice school there will be tensions between social and academic goals, responding to individual differences and creating a sense of community, and professional autonomy and social accountability. Given the complexity of the school community, the approaches to change will require a sophisticated analysis and multi-faceted approach.

Perhaps a critical issue in the change process is to recognise that there is a significant difference between surviving change and mastering change. The fundamental rule of mastering change is to understand that organisations don't change, individuals do. The second rule is that current organisational structures are inappropriate for large-scale change.

The process for change, and the ease with which it can be introduced, depends upon the nature and extent of the change desired. For example, the actual financial costs of changed attitudes to students and parents, improved communication within the school community or the engagement of students in decision making, may be minimal.

However, the resistance to such change within a particular school could be great. The challenge for education systems and schools is to engender the long term commitment required to bring about sustainable change that truly meets the needs of students.

Schools as Learning Organisations

As a way of developing a pro-active perspective towards change, many practitioners, for example Adelman and Fullan, have looked to the work of Peter Senge and the concept of a 'learning organisation'. A learning organisation is one where everyone is striving to continually improve quality through a commitment to ongoing learning. There is now considerable work on the nature of learning organisations across a number of sectors.

The concept of learning organisations is critical when considering the ways in which innovation can develop, thrive and survive in a school environment. At the present time, according to Fullan schools are generally not learning organisations. Learning organisations have structures and processes that enable systematic, corporate or institutional learning by acquiring and building upon new knowledge, reflection and review and then further attempts to improve their practice. Learning organisations absorb new concepts and innovations and quickly adapt to changing conditions which means that they are better able to survive in increasingly turbulent and competitive environments. The features of a learning organisation include:

— Focusing on leadership to develop a sense of purpose and commitment.

— Accurate early identification by an organisation of what is happening, why and the impacts on its clients (students in this case).

— Establishing an improvement process which ensures that there is a ongoing review of policies and processes and the initiation of strategies to redress problems.

— Articulating policies which are supportive of learning and creating an environment where staff are encouraged to take 'reasonable' risks and try out new ideas and innovative strategies.

Learning organisations value staff involvement as a core parameter; staff participation in learning concepts and practices; co-operation among staff and the sharing of expertise; flexibility in organisational structures and work roles; and the development of a staff profile with a broad repertoire of skils, knowledge and experience.

The factors which militate against an organisation developing a learning culture include: lack of time for reflection on experience, funding limitations (and subsequent work pressures) and not using time well for addressing and identifying learning and change needs. School Councils and Boards which are removed from daily learning experiences, and the resistance of individuals and groups to learning and change also can limit an organisation's capacity to learn.

Narrow definitions of training and learning, underplaying the benefit of reflective, experience based approaches, and non-training approaches and lack of planning for staff learning and development are also critical barriers. The need for strong and visionary leadership is a recurring theme in the literature on best practice, and learning organisations.

In the words of Peter Senge the role of the leader is to build learning organisations where people continually expand their capacity to understand complexity, clarify vision and share mental models. In his latest work, which applies the principles of learning organisations to schools and educational system, Peter Senge discusses the key factors which lead to long-term sustainable change in education through schools re-visioning themselves as learning organisations or learning communities.

Through a consultative process engaging a wide range of schools and educational systems, the research team identified processes which have resulted in fundamental shifts in schooling for young people, their families and communities. Again, this research demonstrates that there is a need for local initiatives by parents, teachers, school principals and school boards or councils. Success will be intensified if it is supported at the systems or policy level by strong leadership.

Best Practice

The concept of best practice initially emerged in the business sector, and some of the arguments against applying the concepts of best practice in human services and education have been that the field is not homogeneous and the 'products' are not controllable. There has been a concern that 'best' implies that there is only one right way to do things, which can be applied regardless of the context and circumstances. For this reason the term 'good' practice has found more favour in human service discourse and school effectiveness has been the descriptor that includes research and development that in other fields would be called best practice.

The terms 'exemplary' or 'successful' practice might be more acceptable in education. In the business sector, best practice is a means for setting standards and identifying quality. Increasingly, organisations wishing to differentiate themselves are defining themselves with such terms as 'quality' or 'best practice' or 'client focused'. An organisation which is focused on quality improvement, is future-oriented in considering long term impacts of environmental trends, and uses resources effectively is likely to bring about the best outcomes for those involved.

In practical terms, best practice is elusive—what is best for one organisation is not necessarily best for another. Also, best practices can only be for a point in time—there may be other, better practices just around the corner. Best practice evolves; as an organisation seeks for best practice it must continually strive to maintain the momentum and culture of performance improvement and be ready to change to meet changing circumstances.

However, the concept of best practice, under whichever terminology is adopted, connotes exemplars and new initiatives that work for at risk students. The following characteristics are common across businesses, human service organisations and education settings striving to deliver best practice:

— A shared vision for the delivery of high quality services which is supported by a comprehensive, integrated, and cooperative change strategy to bring about continuous improvement in cost, quality and timeliness.

— A strategic plan, developed through a consultative process, encompassing all aspects of an organisation's operations and setting out short, medium and long term goals.

— A commitment to continuous improvement throughout the organisation.

— Flatter organisational structures supported by the devolution of responsibility, the empowerment of workers, and improved communication.

— A cooperative and participative culture which incorporates effective communication and consultation processes.

— A commitment to continuous improvement and learning, with a highly-skilled and flexible team of workers and recognition of the value of all people in the organisation.

— Innovative human resource policies which include a commitment to occupational health and safety and equal opportunity employment.

—A focus on service users, both internal and external.

The search for ways of describing and measuring quality outcomes is not new for educators, and the need to justify or substantiate both outputs and/or student outcomes has been the subject of considerable debate over recent years.

Research in Canada, the USA and Britain indicates that the concept of best practice is found in schools, although the terminology varies across 'successful., 'effective., 'good., and 'exemplary'. The common characteristics of effective or best practice schools include:

— Productive school climate and culture: orderly environment, staff commitment to achievement, problem solving orientation, staff cohesion and input into decision making, school wide emphasis on recognising achievement.

— Attention to student acquisition of skills: maximising learning time, and emphasis on mastery of skills.

— Monitoring of student progress.

— Onsite staff development and outstanding leadership.

— Keeping parents informed and involved.

— Effective instructional organisation and teaching.

— High expectation and requirements of students.

The principles that are common in effective schools are:

— All students can learn under appropriate conditions.

— School effectiveness depends on the equitable distribution of outcomes across the whole student population.

— Effective schools take responsibility for students and their learning environment.

— The more consistent teaching and learning processes are within the school, the more effective it will be.

These principles, which generally support the findings of Withers & Batten, and Brooks et al on effective programmes, have particular relevance to considerations of good practice with young people who are at risk of leaving school before completion of Year 12 because there is a mind-set displayed which is inclusive of al students regardless of ability and interest, and sees al students as the responsibility of the school community.

Rather than assume that educational quality depends on school wealth and the wealth of students' families, effective schools advocates argue that school success is measured by value added to what students bring with them to the learning process.

Actions of Innovation and Best Practice

Early school leaving severely limits a young person's life choices and opportunities, their development of personal attributes and their access to services. Programs to maintain young people in school occur at a range of developmental stages, and are preventive, interventionist and/or a mixture of both. They are best when they:

— Build relationships

— Reduce individual psychological, physical and behavioural risks

— Reduce family, school and community-based risks

— Build protection by strengthening family relationships, developing relationships with significant others, promoting school belonging, fostering a sense of purpose, and by enhancing pro-social behaviours and problem solving skills.

Student Focused Interventions

Individual Support Strategies

Individual support covers strategies and/or programs that provide targeted assistance in the form of individually tailored responses to the student. The most common are case management, mentoring/advocacy, counselling, tutoring and peer support. Being more time consuming than broad-based programmes, individual support is generally utilised as an intervention strategy for young people who have been identified as being at risk. To be effective, individual support programmes need to:

— assess risks and identify needs;

— provide school-based support as required;

— develop programmes and improve skills; and

— monitor and evaluate.

Cross-Age Tutoring

Cross-age tutoring occurs when an older student supports a younger student (or students) to understand, undertake and complete their school-based tasks on a regular and ongoing basis. Cross-age tutoring has been shown to be an extremely effective strategy with students who are struggling academically and socially.

The Intercultural Development Research Association (USA) is conducting a project which indicates that young people as tutors help the tutored to improve self esteem, increase positive attitudes to school and improve reading grades. The strategy is seen as increasing resilience and connection to peers, the school and community. The protective factors are triggered by three key factors:

- caring and support from another person;
- high expectations in the young person themselves; and
- opportunities for participation in meaningful activities.

The benefits from cross-age tutoring are greatest in structured formats which exhibit:

- careful matching of the tutor and the tutored;
- formal processes;
- adequate resourcing; and
- support and monitoring.

Mentoring

Mentoring may be defined as a sustained relationship between a young person and an adult. Mentors form a one-to-one relationship with a young person where they act as advocate, role-model and/or 'sponsor'. In a well-structured mentoring relationship, the adult provides help, support and guidance. Mentoring may focus on just career advice, or educational progress, but more often it is concerned with holistic personal development. There are mixed assessments about the effectiveness of mentoring programs with a number of evaluations indicating that unless carefully managed they are not successful. Some of the features which should be considered if a programme is to succeed include:

— careful selection and training of mentors;
— time for the relationship to develop;
— regular meetings;
— monitoring and support;
— preparation for programme participants prior to meeting their mentor; and
— structure to define tasks and goals.

One study of 800 student proteges found that more than half reported that mentoring had helped them to learn to succeed, improve their grades, avoid drugs, improve understanding of other races and improve relationships. In addition, the mentors reported positive outcomes for themselves including strengthened family relationships, and recognising that they made a difference.

Case Management

The concept of case management has been developed in therapeutic and welfare settings where individuals require a range of services, often from different workers and institutions. The role of the case manager is to ensure that services are accessible, co-ordinated and monitored. The case manager is usually the person with the greatest contact or the longest involvement with the young person. Successful case management strategies for young people at risk incorporate the following:

— an holistic perspective which views young people in the context of their social family;

— continuity of staff with someone prepared to support the young person over an extended period of time;

— a comprehensive individualised assessment;

— a co-ordinated service plan;

— routine monitoring and follow-up;

— interagency collaboration between school, and the health and community sector;

— time set aside to review practices; and

— documentation.

School-based case management is a more recent strategy. In the school setting effective case management requires a commitment to adequate resourcing including time allowance. Kingsley argues its effectiveness is also dependent on the quality of the relationship between the case manager and the young person and includes:

— Mutual respect between the young person, the case manager, family, other teaching staff and key service providers.

— Each young person only having one service plan. This may involve joint case planning and management across a number of agencies both within the education system and beyond.

— Identification and prioritising of goals.

— A clearly documented action plan.

For maximum impact, school-based case management ought to be orderly and structured, at the same time as being client-centred and flexible. Case management is not for all students since it is time consuming. To improve a case manager's effectiveness, and to help manage the process, many schools have adopted a student support group model.

Counselling

In the school setting counselling may take different forms. This ranges from the communication and helping skills of the teacher, including an understanding of the responsibilities and limits of their role, through to the specialist social worker or psychologist.

The value of teaching support will to some extent depend on:

— developing a caring climate and clear procedures to ensure that students will feel comfortable in discussing their concerns with teachers and with counsellors;

— clearly communicating with students how to obtain the support they need, as well as explaining the teacher's role and what they can and cannot take on when discussing issues;

— knowing how to respond appropriately to student concerns;

— knowing how to raise sensitive issues with parents and how to handle conflicts between students and parents concerning difficulties;

— determining an appropriate level of involvement with students and their families;

— knowing how to communicate with colleagues about particular students, especially when their colleagues have negative attitudes; and

— knowing their professional obligations and accountability requirements, for instance regarding legal issues such as mandatory reporting of child abuse.

Young people find school-based counselling useful when the teacher or counsellor:

— takes time to explain their role and what confidentiality they can offer;

— is a good listener and easy to talk to;

— shows respect and treats the student as an equal;

— gives appropriate information;

— takes further action; and

— has the ability to explore the student's world.

More expert counselling can be accessed through trained welfare workers, social workers and psychologists being located on a school site, through regular school visits or by appointment at community based agencies, health or medical centres.

Peer Support

Peer support occurs when selected students are trained in a range of strategies including mediation, advocacy, counselling and mentoring. It does not have to be particularly formalised, but it is recognised and organised within the school.

Since young people are more likely to seek help from peers than their overseas counterparts, peer education becomes an important strategy. Peer support is different from friendship, although it adds to a student's sense of belonging at school. The potential effectiveness of peer support comes from peer influence, support, credibility, access and empowerment and is based on the premise that young people are more likely to value information that comes from those with whom they can most easily identify.

Peer Education

Peer education is an effective method of building skills and expertise in young people and passing on information to other young people. However, it is a complex process requiring the educator to have expertise in team leading and training as well as content knowledge. Peer education has been used as an intervention strategy in a number of community welfare areas including drug use and AIDS prevention. Its appeal is in the replication of naturally occurring situations where young people learn from each other and is based on the premise that the peer group becomes the key reference point during adolescence.

Although peer education has been shown to be an effective model, there are times when it has failed. According to Walker and Avis the key reasons for this are:

— Lack of clear aims and objectives for the project.

— Inconsistency between the project design and the context in which the program will operate.

— Lack of resources to make the project work—peer education is not a cheap option.

— Lack of appropriate, skilled workers to co-ordinate and manage the project and team.

— Inadequate training and support for the peer educators.

— Lack of clarity around boundaries and control.

— Failure to secure multi-agency support.

There are a number of approaches to peer education and not all of these are effective. Peer education can be defined as young people educating other young people through to professionals providing information in an informal setting where peers interact and take greater control over the content and process.

The first issue in developing a framework for peer education is to clearly define the approach. Some of the questions which need to be addressed include:

— *What do we mean by 'peer'?* While peer education can be defined as sharing experience and knowledge with others who are like us, this does not specify a number of factors, for example age, life experience and educational background.

— *How do we ensure that the peer educators have 'credibility' in the group?* Clearly, in developing peer education programs, there is an expectation that the young people will gain valid information that increases their knowledge and/or skill base and potentially changes their attitudes and behaviour. Some level of credibility needs to be developed through effective training so that the educators are seen as appropriate, by both the young people involved and those who allow access to the program.

— *What are the best methods of sharing information?* Peer education is often seen as an alternative to a didactic approach; however, this does not have to be the case. In early examples young people acted as role models and provided information in very informal settings such as clubs and bars. Other approaches have put young people into a classroom setting where they provide information in a 'semi-formal' manner.

— *What is the role of the adult trainer/co-ordinator/'expert' in the process of peer education?* Do only the peer educators interact with the other young people, or is there a role for the older person?

— *Who controls the content and process?* A key tenet in peer education literature is empowerment. This leads to a set of issues around the ownership and control of the content and process of the peer education program including: Who decides what and how much training the peer educators need? How are decisions made about the content and process? What are the quality and credibility checks from the organisation?

With these questions in mind it is possible to suggest a framework for developing peer education programs.

— *Establishment:* The establishment phase involves research, development of a support team or steering committee; identification of aims, objectives and strategies; clarification of expectations of the processes and outcomes; documentation of philosophy, theoretical and conceptual framework; and preparation of an initial workplan.

— *Building Support:* Consultation with local young people and community groups, health services and schools can build support which is needed to identify potential peer educators and locations for education sessions with young people.

— *Selecting and Training the Peer Educators:* A number of different processes can be used to recruit the peer educators and usually this will involve the network that has been previously developed. Some of the issues to consider in selection include:

  — What age should they be?

  — What other experience do they need?

  — How much support will they need?

  — Who is involved in the process?

— *Ongoing Support, Debriefing and Training:* One of the most critical success factors in peer education programs is the quality and regularity of the debriefing process and the support provided to the peer educators.

Curriculum Initiatives

Curriculum initiatives are those programs and activities that aim to develop or change knowledge, skills and/or attitudes. They can be concerned with cognitive, emotional, behavioural, interpersonal, intrapersonal and physical development. Curriculum initiatives are the main focus of teacher endeavour and debate. Put simply, in their most minimal form these issues are referred to as the

'3Rs':'reading, 'riting and 'rithmetic' Those who subscribe to the view that the purpose of education is solely to teach the '3Rs' are inclined to the view that schools should teach about the basic cognitive skills, about sport and about society's traditional institutions. Health and welfare concerns tend to be the province of family, church and community.

Perhaps the spirit of the contrary view is expressed by Ainley et al who see schools as being involved in shaping young people and their personal, ethical and interpersonal development as three intertwined and important curriculum approaches. In this way, schools not only teach subject matter or develop instrumental skills, they build intrapersonal and interpersonal skills.

All young people are unique. They develop as a whole. The cognitive skills development will not occur in isolation from the behavioural, psychological and attitudinal. Young people learn in a range of ways, using a range of styles, and in a range of stages at a range of speeds. Good practice is student centred and concerned more with learning environments than learning outcomes. The drift towards the latter view seems to be prevailing, albeit schools constantly search for a realistic balance between what they perceive as their minimal obligations (their duty of care) and what they perceive as educational excellence.

Many schools have developed specific learning strategies in an effort to engage and maintain the involvement of at risk young people. Some of these responses are targeted generally at the whole school while many others are specific to particular groups of young people; some focus on literacy and numeracy while others take an integrated approach to curriculum development.

Learning strategies that promote health and well-being are inclusive and flexible, address the range of needs, provide for a range of meaningful opportunities, cater for variety of competencies, give recognition for effort and acknowledge the importance of relationships.

The extent to which learning strategies are preventive and interventionist can be measured by the extent to which they:

— Prevent the emergence of problem behaviours.

— Prevent the escalation (increasing severity and diversity) of problem behaviours.

— Reduce the severity and diversity of problem behaviours already established.

— Enhance protective factors and resilience.

Protective factors can be enhanced in the curriculum context by establishing and maintaining self esteem and self efficacy, and by opening up opportunities of a positive kind. Curriculum that enhances social competence (social skils), problem solving skills, autonomy and sense of purpose and future wil further enhance protection.

The issue of mainstreaming versus special programs is an ongoing area for debate. Many of schools have taken a decision to change the curriculum for the whole school, while others have developed specific curriculum initiatives for targeted groups. In some cases, the targeted group is taken out of the school setting into alternative locations which allow greater flexibility in a more 'casual' learning environment. In very few cases, alternative schools have been established which work only with at risk young people.

Preventive Curriculum Interventions

Pre-School and Early Years Programmes

Prevention is most effective if it occurs early in the child's life and prior to the emergence of problem behaviour; at a later stage prevention aims to stop the escalation of problems.

Literacy is critical to a successful schooling experience. A substantial body of research shows that schools have a narrow 'window of opportunity' in the first 2 years of schooling to make a difference.

Middle Years of Schooling

Middle years of schooling describes a stage of schooling that bridges the traditional 'primary-high school' divide, where students at the pre and early adolescent stage of development are often managed differently by the two levels of the school system.

Effective middle schooling is underpinned by a set of common and agreed upon beliefs and principles, including recognition that young adolescents have particular physical, intellectual, cultural and social needs that are different from those of children and adults. In *Shaping Middle Schooling in Australia: A report on the National Middle Schooling Project*, Barratt, states that, 'the middle years of schooling should provide opportunities for young people to learn and grow in ways that acknowledge and respect this unique phase of their development. The report also identifies learner centred coherent curriculum which is focused on individual needs, interests and concerns of students, and emphasises self-directed and constructive learning. Individual needs include identity, relationships, purpose, empowerment, success, rigour and safety.

Learning strategies include an integrated curriculum framework, cooperative learning, a greater focus on team work with less competition between individuals and inclusive programs that address adolescent interests and concerns, especially health issues and adolescent development.

Curriculum should also be:

— *Relevant*: using practical strategies where possible.

— *Negotiated*: balancing teacher and student choices.

— *Integrated*: connecting students personal and social concerns.

Development of Pro-social Behaviours

While al teachers are engaged in developing pro-social behaviour and attitudes, these aspects have not tended to be included in the formal secondary classroom curriculum. Attitudes and beliefs, social knowledge and skils, problem solving, positive relationships and social action are often canvassed in relation to a range of health and social issues that include drugs, violence, sexual behaviour, body image and diet, through health education and pastoral care programs.

Interventionist Learning Strategies

The more students exhibit behaviours that put them at risk, the more interventionist programmes become.

Risk factors operate at a range of levels; community, school; family and peer/individual. When developing programmes for young people experiencing these risks, programme designers should be aware of the complete context of a student's life, their environment and their social family, rather than just individual behaviours or 'deficits'.

While programmes should continue to aim at reducing risk, connecting young people in positive ways to the community (including employment), family, school and pro-social peers becomes an integral strategy. Marginalised young people are less likely to develop positive social attitudes and behaviours, access support, and where necessary, seek treatment.

Open Learning

Open learning programmes aim to be flexible and accessible. They offer an alternative to classroom learning by utilising a variety of self-paced learning packages, and by encouraging students to decide the pace at which they will learn, where, when and to some extent what they will learn.

Community Based Learning

Community Based Learning isan early leaving prevention strategy. Community based learning involves building community-school partnerships to improve student learning and enhance community development. It covers a wide range of activities including employment, service, advocacy and research. It aims to re-engage young people with education.

Service Learning

Service learning is a form of community based learning which has gained favour in the USA. It is a collaborative learning strategy between schools and the community which combines community service with learning activities. It encourages students to learn and develop through participation in activities that meet community needs. Service learning:

— is integrated into the students' academic curriculum or provides structured time for a student to think, talk, or write about what they did and saw during the actual service activity;

— provides students with opportunities to use newly acquired skills and knowledge in real-life situations in their own communities; and

— enhances what is taught in school by extending student learning beyond the classroom and into the community and helps to foster the development of a sense of caring for others.

The essential components of service learning are:

— Preparation which consists of the learning activities that take place prior to the service itself.

— Action which must meet certain criteria. Each activity must be meaningful; have academic integrity; provide for student ownership; have adequate supervision; and be developmentally appropriate.

— Reflection which enables students to critically think about their service experience.

— Celebration which is the component of service learning which recognises students for their contributions. It also provides closure to an ongoing activity.

The potential of service learning as a 'real dropout prevention. strategy because of the way it counters the following risk factors:

— *Poor academic performance.* As students participate in solving real problems in their communities, the connections with the curriculum begin to make sense.

— *Alienation.* Solving problems with peers as part of a service learning approach can bond these students together and provide the support base so needed by these young people.

— *Low self-esteem.* To actually live the act of being helpful to another person is to gain in self-esteem. The development of social skills used in service learning situations also provides the student with confidence and improved self-esteem.

— *Feeling of helplessness.* By working with adults in service situations, students develop communication and social skills. All of these are prerequisites for successfully becoming empowered.

Organisational Change

Many schools have recognised the need for more fundamental changes than those epresented by individual student focused initiatives. These schools, which take a trategic approach, make changes across the whole school.

Change is an essential aspect of developing effective practice. In fact, to maintain effective practice in schools, change is an on-going process, which ensures an on-going review of policies and processes and the initiation of strategies to address problems. However, change in and of itself does not necessarily lead to good practice. In this ense organisations need to manage the process by developing:

— A shared vision.

— A strategic plan.

— Leadership.

— Commitment from members of the school community.

— Team work.

— Shared responsibilities.

— Cooperation and participation.

— Commitment to occupational health and safety.

In developing a shared vision, it is useful for key players to understand the options available, and their potential effectiveness.

Effective practice in schools includes a productive school climate and culture, monitoring, staff development, parent involvement, effective learning strategies and high expectations. The principles that support this practice include:

— A commitment to the view that all students can learn.

— An equitable distribution of outcomes.

— Responsibility being taken by the school for students and their learning environment.

— Consistency.

For students at risk, efforts that focus on changes across the whole school are often more effective than targeting programmes at specific groups. This approach ensures that young people are not stigmatised and sets a standard that mainstreams expectations of achievement.

For students to develop a sense of belonging at school, they must feel safe and secure and have opportunities for meaningful participation appropriate to their levels of skill, and be recognised for their efforts. Individual support and learning strategies can have a major influence in helping to support and create an inclusive school culture. However, school culture also requires a strategic approach that accounts for the attitudes and actions of all school participants whether they be teachers, parents, students, administrators, maintenance staff and or community workers. How a school develops a supportive and inclusive culture is a difficult issue. One approach which draws from the business sector is personified by the Learning Organisation concept which is being implemented in a number of schools in Canada and the USA.

Features of the Learning Organisation include:

— Focusing on leadership to develop a sense of purpose *and commitment.*

— Accurate early identification of what is happening within an organisation, why it is happening, and its impact on students.

— Ongoing review.

— Articulating policies that encourage innovation.

— Participation.

— Cooperation.

— Flexibility.

— Personnel with a range of skills, knowledge and experience.

The Health Promoting Schools approach is another example of a conceptual framework that provides schools with an organisational structure to develop whole school strategies. In this sense, the Health Promoting School is concerned with the health and well-being of all members of the school community rather than a discrete intervention aimed at a particular target group.

The concept of Health Promoting Schools provides school communities with a set of principles and actions to promote health. In particular a health promoting school can be characterised as a school constantly strengthening its capacity as a healthy setting for living, learning and working.

A Health Promoting School demonstrates an organisational culture that promotes a safe, healthy and stimulating learning environment. It:

— Identifies those health issues specific to the school community.

— Establishes priorities.

— Collaborates with staff, parents, community and students.

— Implements an holistic, co-ordinated and action oriented approach to health.

— Establishes effective partnerships with health services

Developing a vision, a policy and an implementation plan may inform stakeholders about what they would like and how to get there, but it will not always produce the desired outcome. This is because in most change strategies for schools, the only thing that does not change is the people. In spite of all the planning, and the agreements, and the good intentions, what must change is the habits of people, and many of these habits have taken a lifetime to perfect. They do not change just because somebody comes up with a good reason for them to change.

The changing of habits requires motivation, commitment, training, accountability and sometimes, pressure. Classroom activities under the Health Promoting Schools Program in Victoria are designed to teach young people from years P-6 about the qualities that form the basis of healthy relationships. Qualities include, assertiveness, compassion, excellence, friendliness, forgiveness, honesty, kindness, moderation, patience, reliability, self-discipline, tolerance and tact.

Qualities are chosen and students undertake activities and discussion that develops understanding, as well as competence in relation to the quality. The classroom activities are supported by teachers praising behaviours, both within the classroom and outside in the school grounds, which exemplify the weekly qualities. Students are further acknowledged through weekly awards.

The program has proved very popular among primary school teachers. It encourages teachers to examine their own behaviours and how they role model them, and helps them to explore with young people 'what to do., rather than the contrary which is to 'tell' young people 'what not to do'. This approach is just as successful with senior students.

Not only is a health promoting school culture important since it helps create a sense of belonging, but it also provides a point of access to services that may be required by the young person. In fact, for many young people, it may be the only point of access. Many young people have needs that go unnoticed. Schools provide opportunities for identifying young people who are in need of support. While some teachers might believe they do this by using their 'sixth' sense, most commonly the early identification of students at risk occurs through the many forms of communication that teachers have with students and their families. These include:

— The informal chat.

— A visit to the welfare co-ordinator.

— Following up an issue like poor school attendance or erratic behaviour.

— A report from another student.

— A story written by a student or a comment made in class.

— The occurrence of an incident.

Open communication is more likely to occur in a school culture that promotes supportive and meaningful relationships. If students trust teachers, they are more likely to communicate honestly with them, and to seek support when it is required.

Community-oriented Approaches

Franklin and Streeter outline five types of relationships that schools might have with the community in servicing at risk young people:

— informal relations,

— cooperative,

— co-ordination/partnership, —collaboration and
— integration.

Each of these strategies requires a differing level of commitment, training and change or innovation. Dryfoos makes a similar point when referring to 'school-linked' services. She states that they fall along a 'continuum of complexity' and may include:

— Single targeted services such as tutoring provided by a business or organisation.
— Cooperative partnerships in which agencies provide a number of youth specific health services on site.
— Collaborations in which school systems and community agencies redefine their responsibilities, share decision making, and jointly develop a new institution.

School-linked services

Mudaly explains integrated school-linked services as: the provision of co-ordinated health and welfare services for "at risk" children, young people and their families, within local school and community clusters. In other words, a whole school approach to supporting vulnerable and disadvantaged children with a sound community interface.

Lawson and Briar-Lawson argue that school-linked services must not be primarily crisis-oriented, but rather have a preventive focus. If they are seen as being there only to fix problem young people, then they will be neither integrated nor effective.

Informal Relationships

Franklin and Streeter describe informal relationships between schools and the community sector as being those that require little commitment and no change to the organisations involved. Sometimes they require in-service training so the organisations involved have some understanding of each other, their referral procedures and protocols, their job descriptions and professional mission statements, and their differing cultures.

Informal relations often occur in the intervention stage when a student requires resources and expertise beyond the capacities of the school. They are a common relationship. Most schools enter into informal relations with outside agencies at some time. While these types of relationships can be effective, they often remain peripheral to the central activities of the school. Consequently, they tend to attract insufficient resourcing. This creates problems since the young people requiring the intervention are often in need of a level of resourcing above the norm. Frustrations can emerge and young people can receive poor quality care.

Informal relations operate best when a case management plan is operating, and when the school is using some sort of management structure like a school support group.

Cooperative Relationships

Cooperative relationships are similar to informal relationships in their effect on organisational structures. They differ in terms of the level of commitment. some level of formal commitment is made to enter into the relationship. In some instances, the lead organisation in the cooperative relationship may have funding to deliver services to clients of the other organisations.

Co-ordinated Relationships

Co-ordinated relationships require some level of organisational change. Organisations need to undertake meaningful training and make a commitment to the aims of organisational partners. The development of additional programs and resources, as well as the formalisation of pathways into the broader community are potential outcomes of effective partnerships. In other words, informal relationships tend to be reactive liaisons between a school and another organisation, while co-ordinated relationships or partnerships tend to be pro-active.

Collaborative Relationships

Collaborative relationships imply 'change' and 'innovation' in the sense that the participating schools and community organisations need to collaborate in order to achieve something together. Colaborative models are often 'grassroots' initiatives that are informed by a strategic plan that has developed in response to a heightened and broad-based awareness of need; in this instance the needs of young people. They are often, though not necessarily, initiated by the community sector, and in this sense, are community development models for young people. An example of the potential benefits of collaboration between schools and the community sector is demonstrated by the outcomes that have been achieved in the regional centre of Geelong, Victoria.

Integration and Co-ordination Model

It is fundamental to the full service school concept that members of all groups within the school community participate as partners in the development of the vision, the goals, the design and the realisation of the school. These groups include students, families, school-based staff, staff from support services and community members. The participation of parents and young people in planning, implementation and evaluation creates an atmosphere of self-help and ownership.

While the concept of the full service school has grown in response to the perceived needs of children in disadvantaged and high risk areas, there is growing evidence to suggest risk behaviours and circumstances are to be found in all schools. Purpose built full service schools have been developed in the USA to include facilities such as family resource centres, clinics and shops. Clearer definitions and modes of 'collaboration' are currently being devised for the full service school.

Debate about the full service school concept includes such issues as:

— *The location of services:* Some believe services should be located in the schools or at nearby locations. Others argue that effective service delivery requires multiple points of access. Flexibility and innovation will also be limited.

— *The role of the schools:* By locating services in schools, the education sector becomes increasingly powerful at the expense of its collaborative partners.

— *Targeted or universal services*: Who should receive services? Students, families, certain categories of at risk students, or the entire student body? Some of these issues are predicated on views about how scarce resources should be used, while others reflect differing opinions about the extent to which schools should engage in service delivery.

The benefits from full service schools are potential rather than actual at present, though evaluations are under way. The early findings of one evaluation suggested high rates of attendance across the school, high use of all services linked with the school, and high levels of satisfaction among students regarding the school, its services and the prevailing culture.

There are considerable structural and human barriers to implementing a full service school model:

— Entrenched professional identities including differing assumptions, values and beliefs, differing protocols, for example about confidentiality issues, different language, terminology and jargon, lack of a shared agenda, goals and responsibility and differing professional cultures.

— Administration and governance including the need for more complex and more demanding administrative and governance arrangements, extensive time, energy, commitment and skill involved in collaborative decision-making, effects of leadership and staff changes, and the continuing need for development of commitment to the full service school concept in new leaders and staff, as well as the need for different measures of staff accountability.

— Ownership and territoriality including the allocation of space in buildings, the different and competing demands for student time, the allocation of resources, preference of a school to remain focused exclusively on education, fear of one group taking all the power, exclusion of some participant groups from collaboration.

— Funding including the provision of funding for the whole, rather than funding from separate agency resources and financial accountability for the whole program to one body rather than to each separate source agency.

— Change processes including reluctance to see change and be involved in altering current practices, a need for excellent leadership, a lack of sufficient time for undertaking the change process in an optimal manner, a tendency to impose change from the top rather than develop it collaboratively and the need for extensive professional development of all involved.

— Perceptions including the negative effects on school reputation and enrolments if the school is seen as a 'welfare school., as well as a reluctance of young people and families to use services if the services are stigmatised.

The establishment of a full service school is not for the faint-hearted nor for the lukewarm. The need for a managed change process is clearly required if the Full Service School Model is to be implemented and effective. As well as looking for change in students' educational progress, there is also a need to consider:

— changes in children's health development;

— changes in teachers' norms, values and practices, especially in the classroom;

— changes in school structures and culture;

— changes in parents and families; and

— changes in local communities

A comprehensive evaluation should find ways of determining whether true collaboration has been established between the school, community and parents. This should be defined in terms of whether:

— shared goals have been developed;

— responsibilities and accountability are shared; and

— staff work together with one another and with students, parents and community members to achieve the shared goals.

School and Community Change

In this emerging model the underlying philosophy is that the school has a role in regenerating the community and assisting both social and economic growth. The rationale is that for students to learn and grow opportunities need to be available in the broader community. Where these do not exist the school has some responsibility, with the broader community and business to generate them. To date this model appears to have greatest relevance in small and rural communities of 5,000—10,000 population; however, the principles, rationale and strategies have wider relevance.

The case study outlined here demonstrate the following key factors in this model:

— Commitment by the school to all young people and their education.

— Focus on the development and growth of the local community.

— Work at the community level not just the school level.

— Partnerships with parents, community organisations, government departments and businesses to bring about social and economic growth.

— Shared leadership across interest groups to complement each other rather than compete.

— Dedicated resources and people to focus the required changes and implement strategies.

Communities that Care

Another example of schools at the centre of community change is Communities that Care—a prevention approach to building resilience in young people. The Communities That Care Program is an approach that allows communities to demonstrate effectiveness in preventing youth problem behaviours. It is an outcome of work by Professors Hawkins and Catalano of the Social Development Research Group, University of Washington, Seattle.The approach has been adopted in 44 states in the United States of America, as well as in part of the United Kingdom and the Netherlands.

The aims are informed by research in four primary areas:

— *The Social Development Strategy*: young people need to be immersed in environments that consistently enhance protective factors. Young people who have strong bonds to their families, school and communities are more likely to share the beliefs and standards held by these groups.

— *Comprehensive Community-Wide Approach*: guides communities to mobilise all key stakeholders to address youth issues with multiple strategies.

— *Risk-focused Prevention Data-based Predictors*: is a needs analysis tool that identifies risk and protective factors within a community.

— *Promising Approaches*: gives ideas by providing a guide to promising approaches that other communities have undertaken.

The implementation strategy is a five stage process:

— Creating Community Readiness

— Orientation and Involvement of Leaders

— Developing a Data-based Profile

— Developing a Prevention Plan

— Implementing the Plan.

System Change

Social, political and economic systems worldwide, are undergoing extensive and irreversible change; change which is demanding new responses from education systems. However, the real challenge is to prepare students for a dramatically different future and to ensure that each and every one of them has the capacity to cope with what that future might bring.

There are schools around the world that are responding to this challenge. However, individual teachers, principals and even schools cannot make these changes sustainable by themselves. Sustainable change requires support at the systems level through a combination of policy directive and resource commitment, along with significant levels of community and school-based involvement, if education is to assist at risk students to constructively respond to changes in society.

Sustainable change within the system involves change beyond the single local site or initiative. It may include extension of an approach or model across multiple sites, significant expansion of the range of services incorporated within a given model, and can include the structuring of programmatic support services and structures at the school cluster, district, regional, state or national level.

Systemic change requires commitment, resources and support, including monitoring, evaluation and feedback at the site and program levels. Without systemic change, effective practice that serves marginalised young people will mostly remain isolated, and eventually disappear when the personal energy or funding runs out.

Whilst local initiatives may produce small scale benefits, effective models more widely implemented can result in consistent and measurable outcomes for the wider school population. However, balancing local flexibility and responsiveness and broader scale policy goals remains the challenge for educators and policy makers alike. It is difficult, if not impossible to achieve long term sustainable change through short term project-specific funding.

While individual schools may create a different and positive learning environment, which supports the widest range of student need and interest, this is usually dependent on the ongoing energy and enthusiasm of the teachers involved and often disappears when they leave.

Currently, most school-based initiatives aimed at supporting young people at risk are site-specific and reflect a series of specifically targeted interventions. Wardman and Kim advise that most attempts to 'fix' the educational system focus on the individual parts of the system and try to improve them, while believing the goal itself is to fix the broken pieces.

An evaluation study by Wehlage, Smith & Lipman in Withers and Russell indicated that most changes were supplemental rather than fundamental. Re-organisation was often confined to new initiatives being grafted on to the beginning of the school day, such as the introduction of a home-room based guidance period, or at its end, such as the introduction of extended day programs.

The existing models of change management used in education are more appropriate for understanding small-scale innovations than larger reforms. Other interventions, such as 'learning academies' or computer-assisted instruction laboratories, were directed at specific sub-populations of students and remained isolated alternatives rather than models of systemic reform.

What is becoming increasingly evident is that the more comprehensive initiatives, which take an holistic approach to the welfare needs of at risk students clearly overlap with other non-education program areas and this must be considered when assessing cost-effectiveness and outcomes. This requires a systems analysis approach and understanding of the impact of the various interacting influences both on the lives of young people and the education system. From the evidence presented in the literature and the case studies, successful systemic change requires the creation of a vision which touches the lives and hopes of teachers, students, families and the broader community. It also requires the emergence and adoption of a new set of beliefs about the role of schools.

Educational reform includes a broader definition of school leadership, more comprehensive views and prioritisation of results, and an expanded view *on needed change strategies*. Such vision does not necessarily exist amongst specialist technically trained teachers and school administrators. The process by which a vision is developed in a non-threatening and constructive manner becomes critical. Sustainable change can only be achieved when there is clear ownership at the local community service provider level which supports the structural change.

Capacity Building

When schools take on a new and challenging approach to at risk students staff require new skills and expertise. And there is a need for an enhanced range of skills when initiating system-wide innovation that extends beyond traditional teaching and school management or administration knowledge and experience. Edward Joyner describes the need for a new approach to staff development which is consistent with the change processes that will be required at the school and systems levels:

- Mental models are the images and perceptions that inform our day to day decisions and approaches to education, teaching and learning. It is highly likely that many of our current mental models are some of the barriers to changing the system.
- Personal mastery involves learning to hold the vision of a different future in creative tension with acknowledgement of the current reality. Creating the vision is a new set of skills, as is developing the

capacity to hold it in a way that is simultaneously realistic and stretching.

— Team learning is about the quality of relationships both amongst staff and between teachers, students and their families. The case studies demonstrate the power of a positive, consistent and ongoing relationship as the critical factor in bringing about change in the lives of young people.

— Developing shared vision is a highly skilled process and may require both internal and external support.

— Systems thinking and analysis is a skill that has implications at the level of organisational change and as a means of engaging young people in new and exciting ways. Systems thinking is the catalyst of many of the educational initiatives and changes currently occurring in the system.

School boards, parents, members of the general community and collaborating services all need to develop a range of common or complementary skills which recognise the need for the community as a whole to be committed to some form of structural innovation

In their conference report on School Linked Comprehensive Services, the United States Department of Education highlighted several key themes:

— Research on schooling services must apply non-traditional methods in order to capture the complexity of trying to understand the nature of and results from comprehensive services.

— A redesign of research in this area needs to consider two priorities—outcomes for children and families, and the inclusion of clients of programs as contributors to both constructing research agendas and evaluating outcomes.

— The development of leadership for school-linked comprehensive services and of collaborative skills among all of the disciplines involved is an urgent priority.

Implementation and Evaluation

It is rare for new programme initiatives, which are intrinsically complex, to emerge in a fully developed, fully specified and clearly funded form. The pace of change and the need to find locally responsive answers, by definition, implies that there will be a wide diversity of responses and outcomes from ostensibly similar approaches. Indeed there is considerable variation of interpretation of outcomes in the evaluation research. Not only are research results mixed, but also the translation of research results into the improvement of actual schools has been poor.

School effectiveness research has tended to be dominated by the academic community, while school improvement efforts have focused on the knowledge of educators, school self-evaluation and determination of goals by the school. It therefore becomes essential that effective processes are implemented in the early developmental stages of new initiatives which assist in the careful assessment of need, the review of effective interventions, feedback to programme managers and local site managers as well as to communities on findings and developments.

Thornton and Spiesberger designed a manual to assist Californian school personnel to respond to the increasing diversity in student populations, with a change process based on principles of shared leadership through a decentralised site-based management method. The organisation change model utilised by the pilot schools is the California Local Education Reform Network process. They emphasise the need for:

— Organisational readiness and securing district and site leadership commitment to change.

— The site-based management decision to restructure, and clarifying the new roles for participants.

— Orientation stage and needs assessment, selecting a site leadership team, writing a mission statement, and data collection.

— Assessment and diagnosis including analysing the situation, obtaining technical support, and reporting to the school community.

— Quality achievement:

  — prescription (such as organising for planning and building consensus);

  — intervention (converting plans into action and maintaining momentum);

  — evaluation (monitoring dimensions of change and evaluating results); and

— institutionalisation (favourable conditions for institutionalisation and removing institutionalisation barriers).

Sustainable systemic change is rarely achieved without some level of resource input which provides both for the development of skills and expertise, and for any additional infrastructure found necessary to facilitate the continuing operation of such initiatives. A significant criticism of many short-term funded initiatives is that they crumble when the initial demonstration-grant funding is withdrawn. A further criticism of mechanisms of innovation which are programme-specific, is that they fail to offer sufficient flexibility to respond to unique local circumstances, and in particular variability of individual needs of at risk students and young people generally. New programme funding models may be called for which allow for transfer and substitution of resources within and between overlapping programme areas.

Responses to school reform, and the needs of young persons at risk in particular, require complex, flexible and integrated responses. Managing that change requires a system-wide response which supports and resources the change management process on an inter-programmatic basis for extended periods. Effective policy development, and evaluation and feedback is necessary to monitor and evaluate such initiatives.

3

Challenges of Girl's Education

The international community's commitment to universal education was first set down in the 1948 Universal Declaration of Human Rights and later reiterated in the 1989 Convention on the Rights of the Child. At the 1990 World Summit for Children, world leaders not only reaffirmed their commitment that girls and boys alike should have a quality basic education, they also pledged to place their emphasis on reducing the disparities that had existed between rates of school enrolment for decades. Despite these commitments, the ideal of universal education remains unfulfilled and gender gaps persist until today.

The 2005 target date for gender parity is attached not only to the Millennium Development Goals, but to the goals that were first put forth at the World Conference on Education For All in Jomtien, Thailand in 1990, and then reaffirmed at the 2000 World Education Forum in Dakar, Senegal. Here, too, girls' education was afforded first attention: "The most urgent priority is to ensure access to, and improve the quality of education for girls and women, and to remove every obstacle that hampers their active participation...." So it is that for more than a decade, the Education For All (EFA) campaign, led by UNESCO, has embraced a mission that includes both advocacy and "a sense of accountability towards commitments." Through its Global Monitoring Reports, EFA assesses individual countries' yearly progress and champions educational policies that will increase enrolment rates and success in school.

In its 2002 Report, EFA noted that although 86 countries have already achieved gender parity in primary enrolment, and another 36 appear close to meeting that goal, 31 countries, the majority of which are located in sub-Saharan Africa, are at high risk of not achieving the goal by 2015.5 Following Dakar, 13 agencies formed the United Nations Girls' Education Initiative in the EFA spirit to mount a "sustained campaign to improve the quality and availability of girls' education" that works at both the global and country levels.

It is in its capacity as lead agency of this Initiative that UNICEF embraces the urgency of the 2005 Millennium Development Goal to eliminate gender disparity in education. These commitments to universal education and eliminating gender disparities in primary and secondary education by 2005 were avowed once again by the Heads of States and Government who convened at the UN General Assembly Special Session on Children in May 2002 and pledged to make education for all children an essential part of building a 'World Fit for Children'. Despite decades of attention to the issue, some 121 million children are out of school, and 65 million of them are girls. At any moment, they are being denied their right to a basic education, as nations fail to make primary education compulsory, free, available, accessible, acceptable and adaptable to girls and boys alike.And scores of countries are without the talent, energy and creativity these millions of children could bring to the development of their societies.

The two years until the end of 2005 may not seem like much time to those responsible for delivering gender parity by that date. It may seem reasonable to accept that the target is impossible, and to settle for only an incremental improvement. But to that girl the next two years are vital and irreplaceable. Once lost, they cannot be reclaimed. Going to school will transform her life. It will offer her learning and an expanded sense of her own potential, increasing her selfconfidence, her social and negotiation skills, her earning power and her ability to protect herself against violence and ill health.Education will open up the world to her.If the school gates remain shut and barred to this young girl, the gulf between her and the woman she could have become will widen with every passing month. Once she misses her chance to attend primary school, she also loses out on secondary education and beyond. The price of losing two school years would be catastrophic to any child but is even higher for a girl – and it will be paid not only by the girl herself but also by her family, her society and her country.

Whether educated or not, girls are more at risk than boys from HIV/AIDS, sexual exploitation and child trafficking. Without the knowledge and life skills that school can provide, these risks are multiplied. So it is that school allows girls and their families multiple protections and its absence means multiple exposures. Why are girls systematically left out of school, women excluded from political processes, and countries left behind as development advances in some places and not in others?

The following are some reasons:

1. *Failure of accountability.* Rather than recognized as the right of every child, education is too often seen simply as a 'good thing' for most children. As a result, while it is considered desirable to have as many children in school as a country can afford, it is not considered obligatory or necessary that governments mobilize the needed resources so that all children can complete a quality education. Parents often do not realize that governments have the obligation to make education available to all children, and attribute their children's failure to attend school as some failure of their own. They are not likely to demand that governments fulfil this fundamental obligation to their younger citizens. In the face of competing demands on public resources and political will, education loses out. In times of fiscal constraints or social crises – for example, HIV/AIDS and the upheavals that attend violent conflicts or natural disasters – education for some children is easily sacrificed. And because of the persistent and often subtle gender discrimination that runs through most societies, it is girls who are sacrificed first, being the last enrolled and first withdrawn from schools when times get tough.

2. *Failure of understanding.* Human rights principles have not been integrated into economic development programmes, and the ultimate objective of development – human well-being instead of economic performance – has thus been lost. Those who are the most marginalized — women, girls and the poor – lose out the most. Such discrimination, unrecorded, leaves the rights of the marginalized far from the thoughts of development policy makers. In

addition, how educated women contribute to any country's development has yet to be widely recognized. Despite the scientific evidence, educating girls is rarely discussed in policy circles as a way to ensure social progress. As a result, investment in girls' education is often bypassed when budget decisions are being negotiated.

3. *Failure of theory.* Historically, the predominant views of development and the financing mechanisms accompanying them have focused on single-factor motors of development: economic growth and structural adjustment, which underestimate the value of social development, education in general and girls' education in particular. Such approaches do not begin by asking what resources are required to fund education, health, nutrition and shelter for children. They never get to the question of how to raise required resources without destabilizing macroeconomic parameters. The macroeconomic parameters are set first, with resources for people-centred investments, including those that address gender equality, as only a residual consideration. Just as importantly, development paradigms have generally failed to address the unequal relationships between men and women, and failed to take into account women's potential to contribute in the private and public sectors to a country's development. As a result, issues affecting women and girls are nearly invisible in the theories, policies and practices of development.

4. *Failure of strategy.* Even among those committed to the goal of Education For All, there is often a traditional perspective that looks only to the education sector when identifying problems and

> developing solutions. As a result, policies and programmes are often narrow and singlefocused, though it is a multisectoral approach that is needed to overcome the obstacles barring girls from school. Traditional perspectives often fail to take into account the gender issues that affect children's access to school, those related to the differences between the needs of girls and boys, and the inequities in their roles, responsibilities and identities. Without a recognition of such differences, educational policies and practices are gender blind, when they should be gender sensitive. In such cases, the behaviour and attitudes of policy makers and practitioners at best fail to meet the particular needs of boys and girls and at worst sabotage their right to an education.

To successfully remove the barriers that prevent girls from accessing an education, and succeeding in and completing school, societies will inevitably have to deal with factors that are fundamental to the quality of life of the whole community. Girls' education is so inextricably linked with the other facets of human development that to make it a priority is to also make change on a range of other fronts, from the health and status of women to early childhood care, from nutrition, water and sanitation to community empowerment, from the reduction of child labour and other forms of exploitation to the peaceful resolution of conflicts. A concerted global push is now needed to meet the Millennium Development Goals and the education goals of Dakar – as well as to realize the vision of the Special Session on Children to create a world fit for children. The effort is morally imperative; it must also be practical and it must be catalytic. It is within this context that UNICEF's longstanding commitment to girls' education has assumed greater urgency and why we now call on all those concerned with human rights and the Millennium Development Goals to:

1. Accelerate actions in countries that display specific and flagrant gender discrimination against girls and boys, especially in those where either group is significantly at risk of being left out of school.
2. Embrace a human rights-based, multisectoral approach to development, in order to redress the multiple discriminatory situations that deny children their right to quality primary education.

By using a human rights model and a multisectoral approach to ensuring that all girls are educated, the world will necessarily have to address underlying inequities and gender discrimination. The results of such a global initiative will cover a broad landscape. It will create by 2005 a vanguard generation of children who are living a lesson in equality. It will mean that schools, curricula and teachers are changing to become truly child-friendly, thereby offering a better education to all children equally. It will mean that all countries have acknowledged that education is an urgent priority and that developing countries have shifted their resources to attract and retain girls and boys in school. It will mean that donor countries have lived up to their pledges to support development. It will be a powerful global expression of commitment to children's rights.

Benefits of Girls' Education

Education saves and improves the lives of girls and women. It allows women greater control of their lives and provides them with skills to contribute to their societies. It enables them to make decisions for themselves and to influence their families. It is this power that produces all the other developmental and social benefits. Women's participation and influence in governments, families, communities, the economy and the provision of services is a common good. It leads to more equitable development, stronger families, better services, better child health.

Education is a uniquely positive force with a wide-ranging impact on society and human development. Debates continue about whether primary, secondary or tertiary education should be the priority when considering funding for education. But such debates distract from the essential issue for young girls: their right to a basic education. If they miss out on this, they inevitably miss out on secondary education and all the good that goes with it.

Among the many long-term benefits of educating girls are:

Economic Development

Decades of research provide substantial evidence of the link between the expansion of basic education and economic development – and Sonia Yeo/UNICEF/2003 girls' education has an even more positive effect. Regions that invested over the long term in girls' education such as South-East Asia and, at least until the 1980s debt crisis, Latin America, have tended to show higher levels of economic development. As the primary enrolment rate for girls increases, so too does gross domestic product per capita.

Countries that fail to raise the education level of women to the same as that of men increase the cost of their development efforts and pay for the failure with slower growth and reduced income.At the same time, economic development, and hence higher income per family, can help in convincing reluctant parents to forgo the quick economic benefit of their daughters' work, and instead send them to school, producing long-term benefits for a country's economy.

Education for the next generation

If educated girls become mothers they are much more likely to send their children to school, thereby passing on and multiplying benefits both for themselves and society in a positive, intergenerational effect.

One of the clearest findings from a recent UNICEF analysis of household data from 55 countries and 2 Indian states is that children of educated women are much more likely to go to school, and the more schooling the women have received, the more probable it is that their children will also benefit from education.

This recent study backs up research that traces the way in which literacy and language skills gained by girls at school not only result in improved health outcomes for themselves and their children but also eventually for their grandchildren as well.

The multiplier effect

Girls' education is the most effective means of combating many of the most profound challenges to human development. Education is vital in emergencies, following a disaster or when a country is in conflict, contributing stability to the lives of girls and boys and helping families to heal and look forward. For communities, the strategies for providing girls the opportunities to complete their education yield benefits for all.

Education systems the world over have paid a heavy price for the failure of governments to invest in children's earliest years. Like health systems worldwide that struggle desperately to cure illness and disease instead of investing in prevention, teachers and educational experts have wrestled with illiteracy, school avoidance and underachievement – forever playing catchup with problems that would have been significantly reduced if sufficient attention had been paid to children's first years of life.

The neglect of children's early years is by no means confined to education. UNICEF's experience shows that the survival, growth and development of young children are interdependent objectives, achievable only through universal access to a broad range of basic services. Preventing iodine deficiency and anaemia, for example, will improve a child's health and nutrition – and it will also protect a child's early brain development.

Efforts to protect children from violence and abuse will also ensure sound early cognitive development. Ensuring that a woman is empowered, healthy and well educated – a good unto itself – can have a dramatic and positive effect on the well-being of her children, since if she is sickly, hungry or oppressed she is unlikely to nurture her children adequately.

From the understanding that learning begins at birth comes the belief that it can be promoted by a secure attachment and responsive interaction between baby and parents or caregivers. In addition, children's healthy development depends on their interactions beyond their own family, with research suggesting that structured care outside the home can be particularly important in preparing a child for school.

A recent study of children in Nepal showed that over 90 per cent of those who had attended a non-formal pre-school facility enrolled in primary school, compared with some 70 per cent of those who had not. More tellingly still, in grade 2 around 80 per cent of the first group were still in school, but only around 40 per cent of the non-pre-school group were attending.

The same Nepalese study showed that girls benefit even more than boys: 100 per cent of the girls who had experienced non-formal pre-school care enrolled in primary school, 85 per cent of whom were still attending grade 2. There are many possible reasons why girls in particular benefit from pre-school programmes. These benefits include enhanced self-esteem and the raising of their family's aspirations.

Yet one reason that is seldom recognized is that such programmes establish the rhythm of schooling in a young girl's life. In most communities in the developing world, particularly in rural areas, girls are introduced to simple household chores and minor income-generating tasks from a very early age. These tasks gradually become routine, establishing an everyday rhythm in the child's life. Soon, such tasks take up most of the child's day, at which point it becomes difficult to introduce schooling into the routine.

Participation in community-based care, however, establishes a different rhythm, making the idea of regular attendance at a particular time less foreign and daunting. Even spending a few hours each day with a grandparent can help book a place for schooling in a girl's life.

Early childhood programmes can be a vital resource for young women as well as their daughters, and not only because they relieve mothers of their childcare responsibilities. One such project serving Albanian mothers in the former Yugoslav Republic of Macedonia, many of them refugees, has successfully improved participants' parenting skills in ways that will support the physical, emotional and cognitive development of their children.

The programme has encouraged women to read and talk more to their children and to encourage their investigative play and learning; it has helped the women realize their responsibilities as parents and their vital role in child development.In Albania, the Gardens of Mothers and Children community project run by the Christian Children's Fund has successfully mobilized girls who were unemployed and isolated in their homes. The girls work as volunteers who care for, entertain and help educate pre-school-age children.

Fighting HIV/AIDS

Over 5 million people each year are newly infected with HIV/AIDS. Human development gains painstakingly accrued over generations have been wiped out in a matter of a few years in the worst-affected countries. In Botswana, for example, due to the high HIV-infection level, life expectancy plummeted from 60 years in 1990 to just 39 years in 2001.And unless global prevention efforts are significantly expanded, 45 million people in 126 low- and middle-income countries will be infected between 2002 and 2010.

In the absence of a vaccine against HIV/AIDS, education is society's best defence against the disease. The more educated and skilled young people are, the more likely they are to protect themselves from infection; and those who are in school spend less time in risky situations. And girls, who have traditionally had less access to the benefits of education, have an even greater need than boys for the protection that education can provide.

Recent studies confirm that better-educated people have lower rates of infection. A study of 15- to 19-year-olds in Zambia found a marked decline in HIV-prevalence rates among those with a medium to higher level of education but an increase among those with lower educational levels. During the 1990s, the HIV-infection rate in Zambia fell by almost half among educated women, but there was little decline for women without any formal schooling.

A study of 17 countries in Africa and 4 in Latin America showed that better-educated girls tended to delay having sex and were more likely to require their partners to use condoms.The best school-based defence against HIV/AIDS addresses the issue as part of comprehensive life skills programmes, established as a core part of the mainstream curriculum. These offer young people gender-specific information on HIV and on the steps they can take to prevent infection's spread.

The programmes train them to analyse situations critically, challenge gender stereotypes, communicate effectively and make responsible decisions. These skills enhance their abilities to make healthy choices, resist negative pressures and avoid risky behaviour.This is particularly vital for girls, who are more easily infected with HIV during sex than boys.

Life skills programmes also incorporate instruction on health, hygiene and nutrition. Poor nutrition and limited access to safe water and sanitation can compromise the immune system and increase vulnerability to HIV/AIDS and other illnesses.In addition, schools develop a practical link with youth-friendly, gender-sensitive health services that offer voluntary and confidential HIV testing and counselling. The fight against HIV/AIDS then – just like that for girls' education –is multifaceted, and progress on one front cannot be divorced from progress on another.

There are an estimated 11 million children orphaned by AIDS in sub-Saharan Africaand these are often the first children to lose the support of extended families for their attending school. Orphans losing both parents are even less likely to attend school. Girls lose out even more than boys because the burden of care for sick relatives falls disproportionately on them. In many families, HIV-related illnesses and consequent lost earnings make sending a child to school impossibly expensive.

Schools are also suffering due to the illness and deaths of many teachers from HIV/AIDS. In Zambia, around three quarters of the new teachers trained each year are needed to replace those who have died of AIDS. In Malawi, meanwhile, pupil/teacher ratios in some schools swelled to 96 to 1 due to HIV-related illnesses among teachers.

The irony is that school reforms prompted by the HIV/AIDS pandemic often usher in precisely the measures that might otherwise be demanded in the interests of educational quality and child rights. Examples of such reforms include: making school schedules more flexible; holding schools responsible for safeguarding children against sexual harassment; enforcing laws protecting girls from rape and sexual abuse; and empowering children so that they are able to avoid risky behaviour.

In Botswana, which has one of the highest HIV/AIDS adult prevalence rates in the world, and where girls are four times more likely to become infected than boys, the Government is developing and implementing gender-sensitive HIV/AIDS prevention strategies. Some of the strategies include training teachers from hundreds of primary and junior secondary schools on how to run gender-sensitive prevention clubs. There are also plans to prepare hundreds of girls and boys aged 6 to 12 to be peer facilitators in such clubs.

A school improvement project is strengthening life skills education and making schools more gender-sensitive, child-friendly and responsive to children's psychosocial needs. In Uganda, *Straight Talk,* a monthly newspaper for adolescents that addresses HIV/AIDS in relation to sexuality, feelings and values, is distributed to schools, churches and communitybased organizations. The paper is mailed to over 3,000 addresses inside and outside Uganda, almost half of which are secondary schools. In Namibia, students aged 14 to 21 are being prepared to educate their peers on ways to protect themselves from pregnancy, HIV/AIDS infection, substance abuse and rape. Schools now being targeted have reported a decline in the number of pregnancies and dropouts.

Making a Protective Environment

After families, education is the next perimeter of a protective environment for children. Schools can be a powerful protective force in most children's lives, especially for girls and others who are highly vulnerable. This is not only because schools physically remove children from potential harm for much of the day but also because they help children learn skills and gather information so that they can protect themselves.

Education remains a key safeguard preventing child labour and helping to combat the sexual exploitation and trafficking of children, which mainly threatens girls. A girl who is in school is less likely to be drawn into exploitative forms of work outside the home –and is also drawn away from domestic duties that may be excessive.

Girls who are literate, and particularly those who have gained greater confidence through life skills training, are less vulnerable to the extreme forms of intrafamily violence, sexual exploitation and trafficking. The millions of children who are exploited each year are living proof of the world's systemic failure to protect its youngest citizens.

According to the International Labour Organization, every year an estimated 1.2 million children are trafficked into forced labour or prostitution. A recent UNICEF survey of households in 25 sub-Saharan African countries indicated that 31 per cent of children aged between 5 and 14 are engaged in the unconditional worst forms of child labour that should be eliminated, such as slavery, trafficking, and forced recruitment for the purposes of armed conflict, prostitution and pornography; and that 9 per cent are engaged in hazardous work, that is, working more than 43 hours a week in labour that threatens their well-being. In the countries surveyed, there are an estimated 31 million child workers, 24 million child labourers and 7 million children involved in hazardous work.

More girls were found to be engaged in hazardous work than boys because household chores of more than four hours per day were taken into account. Ultimately children will only be free from child labour, trafficking and sexual exploitation when:

— Governments make child protection a priority

— Discriminatory attitudes and practices towards children are challenged and changed by the media and civil society

— Laws are in place and reliably enforced

— Teachers, health workers, parents and all those who interact with children know how to recognize and respond to child abuse

— Children are given the information and knowledge they need to protect themselves

— Adequate monitoring systems are in place to document or highlight the incidence of abuses

— Gender equality and women's rights are ensured.

In Bangladesh since 1997, schools for the hard to reach, using the BRAC model, run for two hours each day, six days a week, and are drawing in children such as girls living-in as domestic workers, who would otherwise have no chance to receive a basic education.In Morocco, according to a 2001 survey by the Ministry of Economic Provision and Planning, about 23,000 girls were employed as maids in the Grand Casablanca region, some 60 per cent of them under 15.

Since 2001, in partnership with local non-governmental organizations, and supported by the Wilaya of Casablanca, UNICEF has helped these girls receive an education and basic health care. This intersectoral programme also seeks to eradicate the problem at its root by publicizing the harsh reality of these girls' lives.

Advantages of Gender-sensitive Education

Education is not a luxury item that is only to be ensured in an emergency once other elements are in place; it should be given priority and started as soon as possible. Girls are especially vulnerable in emergency situations – and they must be especially protected against physical, sexual and psychological abuse. This means establishing safe environments in which girls as well as boys can learn, play and receive psychosocial support.

The goal is to create a child-friendly space, a concept that was developed during 1999 in response to the Kosovo crisis, the earthquake in Turkey and the violence in what was then East Timor (now Timor-Leste). Since then, the concept has been applied through the Learning Tree Initiative in several other conflict situations, such as in Guinea, Liberia and Sierra Leone. Programmes include vocational training, teacher training for psychosocial support, school books and benches, and, in the case of Guinea, building a school.

In Liberia, the Support to War Affected Youth project aims to catalyse the leadership potential of 10,000 Liberian youth by ensuring access to basic education and social services. Using art, sport and recreation as entry points for recruitment, the programme now includes HIV/AIDS prevention and integrated child development services for children of teenaged mothers enrolled in vocational training programmes.

Amid the chaos and trauma of an emergency situation it is still possible to put children's rights first; in some circumstances it can even be a window of opportunity to meet previously unmet needs. Within the refugee settlement a safe area is set up in which tents or other temporary structures are erected in a broadly circular pattern, with a water point and a space for play in the centre, and zones for schooling (both pre and primary), mother-support, and provision of primary health care and psychosocial support on the outside.

A child-friendly, gender-sensitive space makes it possible for:

— All schoolchildren to continue their respective school cycles

— Parents to undertake their own activities knowing that their children are in a caring, safe environment

— Young mothers to spend private time with their infants and receive counselling necessary for their healthy development

— Mothers and young women to continue their own education

— Young people to be trained as service providers for children.

In southern Sudan, which has been blighted by civil war for decades, to wait for an end to the conflict would be to dismiss the rights of generations of children. UNICEF, working with the Sudan People's Liberation Movement/ Army in areas it controls, is trying to address the dire educational position of children: As few as 15 per cent of primary-school-aged children in southern Sudan are in school, and girls represent only one quarter of this number.

By the time the upper primary level is reached, there are hardly any girls left in school and at the territory's foremost secondary school, Rumbek, there is a solitary girl. Only 560 of the 8,000 teachers in southern Sudan are women, a mere 7 per cent.

The benefits to communities Efforts to get more girls into school also benefit the development of whole communities. For example, it has long been recognized that if a poverty-stricken household is forced to choose which children it can afford to send to school, girls will often lose out. Yet education-prompted measures designed to address this disparity by boosting household income benefit the whole family and the local community – particularly if the extra income is channelled towards the mother, who is more likely than the father to invest it in the needs of children and the family.

Similarly, girls tend to suffer more from poor nutrition; in families with scant resources they are often given substantially less food than boys. Thus girls benefit even more than boys from school-feeding programmes. Malawi's school-feeding programme, considered a particularly important factor in keeping girls in school, currently reaches about 160,000 children in eight districts. Such programmes –along with accompanying messages about healthy eating – can also trigger better nutrition practices within families, thereby improving the health and well-being of the whole community.

Safe water and sanitation is another key area in which the whole community can benefit when a 'gender lens' is applied to education. The absence of safe water and separate toilets can be a major reason why girls never attend school –or drop out of school, particularly at puberty. Providing adequate sanitation facilities has, as a result, assumed a much higher priority within girls' education programmes. The drive to get more girls into school, then, can transform the quality of life in a local community, which may have for years made do with polluted, distant water sources or no sanitation at all.

In the Lao People's Democratic Republic, for example, the lack of access to water and sanitation is a major factor influencing poor school attendance and learning. More than a fifth of girls nationwide are not enrolled in school and in some areas the rate is more than 50 per cent. The issue is not just the lack of facilities in schools, but their absence in the wider community.

Unhealthy children cannot go to school as often as they should and do not learn as effectively when they are there. Infection by parasites that consume nutrients and thereby aggravate malnutrition and retard development is particularly high in Lao PDR, affecting as much as 62 per cent of children in some regions.

In addition, the household chore of fetching water falls mainly to girls, who can spend as much as two hours a day on the activity, using up one third of their daily caloric intake in the process. Even those who make it to school may be sent by their teachers to fetch water, further impeding their learning.

To address this issue, the Ministries of Health and Education have focused on primary schools and surrounding communities in eight remote and poor provinces.

New water points and latrines are being constructed in schools and surrounding villages; deworming activities are being carried out; and a hygiene-education campaign is being launched, mobilizing not just teachers but also children as hygiene promoters within their communities. The project will reach 300 schools and 70,000 pupils, providing access to safe water and sanitation for 18,000 families in 350 communities.

Impacts of Economic Disparities

Although the international community has committed itself to girls' education as a human rights issue and the benefits of investing in girls' education are clear, it has yet to become a priority for development investments. The reasons for this are complex and bring into question not just education policy but the historically dominant approaches to development that prioritize economic considerations and ignore human rights.

Many of the early ideas about development were rooted in the belief that economic growth, measured by gross domestic product, was paramount. It was assumed that as the total value of goods produced and services provided by any country within one year expanded, poverty and inequality would be automatically, almost magically, reduced. The fruits of economic growth, it was assumed, would fall into the laps of all, whether rich or poor, male or female.

This view of growth as central to development in a country's productivity was refined and redefined frequently as many years of dismal experience in developing countries proved the model's inadequacy. Growth remained limited in all but a few developing countries and no consistent evidence emerged to show that this type of growth alone would reduce poverty or inequality.

The economics of development at this point were also gender blind. There was no attempt to consider if or how the status of women relative to men affected their participation in economic development. It also ignored areas of the so-called 'unpaid care' economy, i.e., domestic, nursing and other nurturing work largely undertaken by women on whom the 'productive' sector of the economy depended. There was also little awareness that any benefits accruing to a household may be distributed unequally due to the established power relations between men and women.

In the 1980s, as growth models faltered, the World Bank and the International Monetary Fund spearheaded the implementation of structural adjustment programmes aimed at reducing public expenditure and giving more scope for prices and incentives to find their own level in the marketplace. Adjustment often entailed cuts in spending on education, health and food subsidies that disproportionately hurt the poor.

These cuts hit poor women particularly hard since they had to step up their workload both inside and outside the home so that their families could cope. Adjustment also failed even on its own terms, resulting in next-to-no economic growth. Per capita growth in developing countries plummeted even as adjustment lending by the Bank and the Fund soared.

A Bank study in 2000 concluded: Growth of per capita income for a typical developing country during the 1980s and 1990s was zero. By the 1990s, the assumption that economic growth alone would deliver human development was recognized as flawed. The opposite seems to be true: human development can foster economic growth.

A UNICEF study of 49 nations shows that the countries that achieved the highest average annual growth between 1990 and 2000 were those that had a baseline in 1980 of low child mortality and low income poverty; while the economies that actually shrank in that decade were those that all started in 1980 with high child mortality, high income poverty or both.

There is now a more general acceptance that development, if it is to be meaningful, has to transcend economics. There is also more widespread understanding – particularly since the Platform for Action at the Fourth World Conference on Women in Beijing in 1995 – that a gender perspective on the economics of development is essential, and that poverty cannot be reduced in any sustainable manner without promoting women's empowerment.

Education policy has followed a slow path to the realization that girls' schooling is fundamental to a country's success in achieving education for all. In the early years of the development movement, when many countries were newly independent, there was general enthusiasm for education as a vital factor in a nation's advancement. But the task of educating all children was huge.

In 1960, fewer than half of the developing world's children aged 6 to 11 were enrolled in primary school, and in sub-Saharan Africa only 1 child in 20 attended secondary school. And by 1980, despite some success (overall primary enrolment had doubled in Asia and Latin America, and tripled in Africa) millions of children were still out of school, the majority of them girls. Rapid population growth consistently frustrated progress, staying ahead of the increase in the numbers in school. In the 1980s, structural adjustment made things worse.

A study of the sub-Saharan countries that underwent adjustment between 1980 and 1993 indicates that the average reduction in real per capita spending was 14 per cent during the adjustment period.Of the 15 countries in this group, 12 had a decline in per capita spending on education.

In 1990, the World Conference on Education For All held in Jomtien, Thailand recognized the chronic neglect of children's right to education in the poorest countries, especially the neglect of the rights of girls which, under structural adjustment in the 1980s, was exacerbated rather than mitigated by international intervention and concern. This landmark gathering took a major step towards refocusing the world's attention, making high-quality primary education the cornerstone of its renewed drive to put all children in school. It served to re-establish education at the heart of development.

Models for Girls' Education

The Jomtien Conference, and the Education For All movement that was born of it, recognized the importance of closing the gender gap and of taking special measures to enable girls to go to school and to stay there. In the laudable drive towards education for all, it was assumed that the gender gap would be automatically reduced. In reality, this was not necessarily the case.

The greater attention paid to girls' education throughout the 1990s can be attributed to the intersection of two key movements based on human rights: the child rights movement that gathered steady momentum in the wake of the adoption of the Convention on the Rights of the Child in 1989, and the women's movement, which culminated in the Platform for Action at the 1995 Fourth World Conference on Women in Beijing, a platform specifically addressed to the needs and rights of girls.

In this sense it has taken until the 21st century for girls' education to receive its due primacy. The academic evidence and programmatic proof of its efficacy had been there for many years, certainly since the late 1980s and early 1990s. But it was only in 2000, at the UN Millennium Summit and the World Education Forum in Dakar, that the push for girls' education moved from the education sector to centre stage.

Beyond these broad international trends are other factors that have stopped girls' education from garnering the attention it deserves. Local beliefs, cultural practices and attitudes to gender roles, such as whether education improves or reduces a girl's chance of marriage, can undoubtedly hold girls back from school.

Cultural resistance is not always consistent in all countries and may vary in specific parts of a country or with specific population groups. What's more, expectations about gender roles differ at different stages of the life cycle, as in many Latin American and Caribbean countries, where there are marked differences between the early years of primary school and late adolescence.

But parents' objections to their daughters going to school are more likely to be on the grounds of safety or economics than out of a belief that girls should not be educated. They may feel that a school is unsafe, or that the journey to school is perilous or too long, putting girls at risk of sexual assault or other forms of violence. Too often their feelings are right on target.

Alternatively, they may believe that sacrificing a daughter's work at home or in the fields would jeopardize family income and survival. For poor families, bearing the opportunity cost of sending a girl to school may not seem economically justifiable in the short term. This is especially the case in societies that have not embraced the idea that women have the right to paid employment or where jobs for educated women are scarce. Decisions about whether to send daughters to school are often taken on the basis of analysing the costs and benefits to the whole family.

In these cases the problem is often more on the supply side – the availability of safe, accessible and girl-friendly schools; employment possibilities for women; educational information for parents – than with any lack of demand for education from families. The proportion of parents who would stand against their daughters being educated, once the benefits had been convincingly explained and the physical or economic barriers at the local or family level had been overcome, would be small indeed.

In Sierra Leone, for example, in areas where communities have been trained to work together on issues of common concern, parents, including very poor ones, now send their daughters to school.When the Kenyan Government announced in 2003 that education fees were abolished, the schools were flooded with 1.3 million children and adolescents who had previously been excluded. Of these, nearly half were girls.

The sense that the primary problem is not with the lack of demand for education from children and their parents is reinforced by opinion surveys from around the world.

According to a recent global survey by the Pew Research Center, 6 in 10 respondents in Latin America and more than one half of Africans see poor schools as a "top national concern."When the polling organization Gallup International interviewed more than 50,000 people in 60 countries, 86 per cent of those surveyed rejected the suggestion that education was more important for boys than girls.

In the same vein, a recent World Bank comparative study of 23 countries carried moving testimonies from parents in poor families strug-gling with the decision as to whether to invest in their children's education – and from others already making heartbreaking sacrifices in order to do so.

An extensive UNICEF survey of children and adolescents in East Asia and the Pacific asked those not attending school for their reasons. Only 19 per cent responded that they did not want to go to school or did not like school. Some 22 per cent had stopped school so they could work.

While 43 per cent reported being out of school due to lack of money, 22 per cent cited the necessity of helping at home and 4 per cent said there was simply no school available. Furthermore, by far the most popular priority in the Say Yes for Children campaign, which amassed nearly 95 million votes of support from adults and children worldwide from 2001 to 2002, was "Educate every child."

Given this demand from the grass roots, the main 'cultural resistance' may be the reluctance of national and international policy makers to make education a priority and to implement measures that have been shown to work on the ground. The special situation of girls and women has traditionally been 'invisible' to predominantly male policy makers and girls' education as an issue is only now being brought into the light.

In some powerful quarters there will still be overt discrimination and determined resistance to the idea of giving girls an equal chance. Many politicians, administrators or aid officials who pay lip service to the principles of gender equality remain uncomfortable with programmes that have a specific gender focus, and passively fail to implement them.

Any drive to get all girls into school has to be sensitive to the local context. It has to squarely face up to the realities of gender discrimination, wherever it exists. 'Traditional culture' is often used as an excuse to explain why expected results in girls' education have not been achieved. Increasingly, that excuse does not stand up to scrutiny.

A recent report on the extent and depth of child poverty in the developing worldfound there to be some 135 million children between 7 and 18 years old without any education at all, with girls 60 per cent more likely than boys (16 per cent compared with 10 per cent) to be so 'educationally deprived. Practically all children who are deprived of an education also suffer other deprivations.

Thus, the stark disparity between genders relative to education translates into the probability that girls are more likely than boys to endure other manifestations of poverty, such as being deprived of food, safe drinking water, sanitation facilities, health, shelter or information. What's more, although the gender disparity in education is apparent for both the poor and non-poor alike, it is significantly greater for children living in poverty (12 per cent of boys and 17 per cent of girls) than for those living above the poverty threshold (3 per cent of boys and 5 per cent of girls). Thus, girls are in dou-ble jeopardy: because of their gender and because of their poverty.

A Human Rights, Multisectoral Model

There is an alternative approach to development that will allow girls their right to education, meet the commitments of the international community and maximize the multiplier effects of investing in girls' education – a human rights, multisectoral model.

Human Rights

The successful efforts to have the United Nations adopt such an approach were led by UNICEF, whose work and mission are based on two fundamental human rights treaties: The Convention on the Rights of the Child and the Convention on the Elimination of All Forms of Discrimination against Women. Since 1996, UNICEF has been guided by the principles of these two treaties, linking the rights of children with the rights of women in all its programmes of cooperation.

Within this context, it is understood that children's rights cannot be realized nationally or globally without addressing discrimination in all its forms, especially the specific situation of girls and gender-based discrimination. And further, when the human rights principles of universality, equality, non-discrimination and participation are applied in economic approaches to development, the result is more equitable, democratic and sustainable growth for all.

Multisectoral

Many, some would say most, of the obstacles that keep girls from enjoying their right to complete their education are found far from the school room. In towns without access to water, in communities sieged by HIV/AIDS, and in families caught in poverty's grip, girls are often kept at home to fetch daily rations, care for siblings or serve as domestic workers. In the face of such challenging realities, no new curriculum, gender-sensitive lesson plan or culturally appropriate textbooks will get them to school.

Solutions must come from outside education's standard framework – from an approach that integrates planning and action across multiple sectors. For example, interventions in health and nutrition, although initially designed to improve a child's chances of survival and sound development, will also contribute to better performance in school. Providing school meals will improve a child's nutrition, and also provide an incentive for youngsters to enter and stay in school. Logically and inevitably, a multisectoral approach will yield the greatest results for girls' education.

Gender Gap in Education :Consequenses

The Millennium Development Goals aims that by 2015, all boys and girls alike should have access to, and complete, a good quality primary education. 'All' implies that girls and boys must be equally well provided for; but there is a separate Millennium Development Goal that makes this explicit: to eliminate by 2005 all gender disparity in primary and secondary education, and to achieve by 2015 full gender equality in education – including enrolment, completion and learning achievement. But these goals look dauntingly distant.

Access to primary schooling is most usefully measured by net enrolment ratios. These increased during the 1990s in all regions and made for a world average of 81 per cent enrolment by 2002. But the regional variation is enormous. While enrolment rates in Latin America and the Caribbean are close to those in industrialized countries, at 94 and 97 per cent respectively, South Asia lags much further behind at 74 per cent, while sub-Saharan Africa languishes at a mere 59 per cent.

Every year an increasing number of children have been accommodated within primary education, but available places are not sufficient to keep pace with the annual growth in the school-age population. As a result, the global number of children out of school stubbornly remains undiminished at 121 million – and the majority is still girls. This failure to reduce the overall number of children who do not attend school is worrying enough – especially bearing in mind the hazards, from exploitative child labour to HIV/AIDS, to which these out-of-school children are disproportionately exposed – but the global figure hides an even more disturbing truth at the regional level. Sub-Saharan Africa, for example, accounts for a proportionately larger number of the world's non-enrolled primaryschool-aged children – 41 million in 1990 and 45 million in 2002. Significantly, the mass of children out of school includes those who have dropped out early, as well as those who have never set foot in a classroom.

The Millennium Development Goals specify that the world needs to ensure that children complete their primary schooling –it is not enough that they merely register and attend only for a year or two.

A recent World Bank study indicates that the population-weighted rate of primary-school completion in the developing world rose from 73 per cent to 81 per cent during the 1990s.Again, the global figure masks great regional and gender variations. In sub-Saharan Africa the completion rate has improved over the decade but it is still barely over 50 per cent, and if it continues to increase only at the present rate, it will barely reach 60 per cent by 2015. In the Middle East and North Africa completion rates are generally higher, at around 74 per cent, but have remained stagnant throughout the 1990s.

In many cases, out-of-school girls are 'invisible'; they are either not reported or underreported. Many countries suffer from a real information gap in which populations in hard-to-reach areas are often not accounted for. In addition, countries mostly report on averages and thus frequently conceal very serious gender disparities between internal regions, and economic and ethnic groups. The same study indicates that if the rate of progress in the 1990s extends to 2015, nearly one child in five will still fail to complete primary school.

Girls Drop-out

The gender gap in primary school enrolment certainly narrowed during the 1990s. The ratio of girls' gross enrolment rate to boys' in developing countries increased from 0.86 to 0.92. Nearly two thirds of developing countries improved on girls' enrolment over the decade, with the biggest improvements seen in Benin, Chad, the Gambia, Guinea, Mali, Mauritania, Morocco, Nepal, Pakistan and Sudan.

In Morocco, the proportion of girls' enrolment in rural areas shot up from 44.6 per cent in 1997–1998 to 82.2 per cent in 2002–2003.Yet girls' primary school completion rate still lags way behind boys', at 76 per cent compared with 85 per cent. This yawning gender gap means that millions more girls than boys are dropping out each year.As a result, the majority of the children not in school are girls.

The most worrying statistics come from sub-Saharan Africa, where the number of girls out of school rose from

20 million in 1990 to 24 million in 2002.Eighty-three per cent of all girls out of school in the world live in sub-Saharan Africa, South Asia and East Asia and the Pacific. The latest UNICEF global figures, which include both girls' attendance and enrolment, show that 70 countries have rates of less than 85 per cent. This highlights the need for urgent, targeted action. Most countries reduced the gender enrolment gap in secondary education during the 1990s.

The countries with the smallest proportion of girls enrolling in secondary school are, with the exception of Bhutan, all in sub-Saharan Africa; in Burkina Faso, Burundi, Chad, Ethiopia, Guinea, Niger, Somalia and the United Republic of Tanzania the gross enrolment rate is under 10 per cent.This region also has few female teachers – less than one in four in some countries– though even here the proportion of female teachers is increasing. In two thirds of the Arab states women now make up at least half of teachers, while in Latin America and the Caribbean they account for 80 per cent of staff.

In Bosnia and Herzegovina, as in other countries in the Central and Eastern European region and throughout Latin America and the Caribbean, issues related to girls' education constitute a 'hidden crisis'. Since there are good attendance and enrolment rates among girls, their education is not seen as a concern, even though reports on the increasing number of girls who drop out of school, especially in rural areas, are an indication that a serious problem exists. In the past decade, enrolment rates in some countries in the Central and Eastern European region have decreased considerably at all levels from preprimary to secondary.

Moreover, parity in enrolment does not equate to parity in education, which also includes completion and learning achievement. In many cases, countries might show no enrolment gap between boys and girls but a serious gap in learning achievements, reflecting a difference in the quality of education received by girls and boys. In Serbia and Montenegro, although general statistics are not alarming, data show that girls who are discriminated against due to poverty, developmental disorders or ethnic background (like the Roma) suffer a double disadvantage when it comes to access to education. Their drop-out rate is reported to be up to 80 per cent higher than that of boys.

In Azerbaijan, a survey conducted in 2002 revealed a gender gap in learning achievement in terms of literacy, numeracy and life skills among children leaving primary school. While all of the boys passed the literacy test, only 52 per cent of the girls passed. All boys passed the numeracy exam, while only 52 per cent of girls were successful. All boys were successful in a life skills test, while only 72 per cent of girls passed. Clearly, participation in education itself is not necessarily an empowering activity. Stereotypes can actually be reinforced by participating in a system where traditional gender roles are being taught, lowering girls' sense of their own potential and their learning achievement.

Even when girls' enrolment and completion rates are higher than those of boys', girls may not advance beyond primary and secondary education, women are not found in leadership roles, and qualified women too often still earn less than men. The challenge for the countries that have achieved gender parity is to identify ways to expand the family and societal perception and expectations of girls' capacity – such as a push for greater participation in tertiary education and more leadership roles. These countries are ready for the societal transformation to help them make the leap and to further advance girls' participation in society.

Shortage of Funding

None of the world's wealthier countries developed without making a significant investment in education. For example, Japan's emergence as a major economic power in the first half of the 20th century is attributed by many to the emphasis it placed on education and literacy. Between 1906 and 1911, education consumed as much as 43 per cent of Japanese town and village budgets.More recently, the spectacular economic growth and poverty reduction seen in many East Asian countries in the last quarter of the 20th century has been attributed in good part to sustained investment in education.

If the spirit of the Millennium Declaration and the targets of the Millennium Development Goals are to be met – and the education goals are only one part of the picture – it is clear that governments in developing countries will have to bear the lion's share of the responsibility. Many are already investing more in human development than ever before, but across the board there has not been the major shift of resources into education that is required.

Only eight developing countries in the period 1999 to 2000 committed more than a fifth of their government spending to education: Côte d'Ivoire (40.8 per cent), Togo (26.2 per cent), Malaysia (25.2 per cent), Azerbaijan (24.4 per cent), Comoros (23.5 per cent), Mexico (22.6 per cent), Saint Lucia (21.3 per cent) and Peru (21.1 per cent).

It is also true that despite some significant exceptions, industrialized countries and international financial institutions have so far substantially failed to meet their part of the bargain. In 1990, both at the Jomtien Conference and the World Summit for Children, donor countries promised extra funds for education. In 1996, they made an additional commitment to ensure universal primary education by the year 2015.

Instead, total aid flows to developing countries actually declined during the 1990s, from a peak of $60.6 billion in 1991 to $49.6 billion in 2000, a reduction of 18 per cent. No one could doubt that the greatest need in this period lay in sub-Saharan Africa, yet total development assistance to the region shrank by 14 per cent in real terms between 1990 and 2000, at the same time that aid to the East Asian region grew. Bilateral funding for education has plummeted even further, with a general decline through the decade followed by a dramatic cut in 2000 that left aid at $3.5 billion – a full 30 per cent lower than in 1990. World Bank International Development Association loans to education, which averaged $0.9 billion per year from 1990 to 1996, averaged only $0.6 billion between 1997 and 2001, a cut of 33 per cent.

There are recent, tentatively hopeful, signs that the climate for development assistance is changing, partly as a direct result of the commitments represented by the Millennium Development Goals. A new consensus on investing in education emerged at the International Conference on Financing for Development in Monterrey, Mexico in 2002, and education forms a vital part of the 'World Fit for Children' commitments made at the UN General Assembly Special Session on Children that same year. Governments, including those in the G-8, have pledged to increase their overall aid, particularly their aid to basic education. The World Bank has launched the Fast-Track Initiative – a venture that could help transform the Education For All landscape.

Plight of Boys' Education

All children benefit from the expansion and development of integrated early childhood programmes. Similarly, while scheduling lessons flexibly so as to include children required to work in the home or the family fields may benefit girls most, it also makes school possible for boys all over the world who work either in or outside their home and would otherwise be denied the opportunity. When schools are located closer to children's homes it makes them more accessible to girls and renders the journey to school less of a concern for them and their parents – and it makes getting to school easier for boys, too. The same applies to the provision of water and latrines in schools, or to ensuring the care and maintenance of school buildings.

A violence-free school environment is also of clear advantage to boys as well as girls since the school playground can be a brutal place in which physical weakness is exploited and outsiders can be victimized and bullied. With this in mind, making schools safe is a cause pursued as passionately on behalf of boys as of girls. More fundamentally still, a key element in advancing girls' education is the development of child-friendly, gender-conscious teaching methods that reach out to children's individual needs.

Girls may need this change in educational approach more than their boy peers, but what it translates into is better, more sensitive and child-centred teaching for all children, and an improved learning experience for boys as well. An extensive evaluation by USAID in eight countries concluded that boys have consistently benefited from programmes and policies to improve girls' education.Not only did boys as well as girls benefit from initiatives to improve school quality, but boys' enrolment also increased together with that of girls.

Boys face many of the same problems as girls: restricted access, poor quality, lack of nearby schools and the absence of parental support for education. When these are addressed in order to get more girls into school, boys – especially those from vulnerable or marginalized groups – also reap the reward. To a large extent, the cause of developing gender-sensitive education systems worldwide benefits boys as well as girls. Nevertheless, it is important to recognize that in some countries and regions – including much of the industrialized world – it is boys' academic underachievement and disaffection with school that are causing concern.

Boys Left-out

In a minority of countries, there are fewer boys than girls enrolled in school. A recent UNICEF study of household data from 55 countries confirms that while in a clear majority of countries girls' attendance at school is far lower than boys', in some countries boys are the ones not being reached by the education system.

In countries such as Botswana, Lesotho, Mongolia and Namibia, this is largely due to a practice of having boys look after family cattle while the men seek wage-earning work. But in most parts of Latin America and the Caribbean, which has no such ingrained pastoral tradition, the same underperformance and even disappearance of boys is evident in the school system.

In Latin America and the Caribbean, boys generally have higher repetition rates and lower academic achievement levels than girls, and in some countries, a higher rate of absenteeism. In Brazil in 1996, men had an average of 5.7 years of formal education compared with 6.0 years for women. Gender disparity starts to show up around age 10 for boys, when they begin to leave school at a higher rate than girls. At ages 15 to 17, 19.2 per cent of boys have dropped out altogether, compared with only 8.5 per cent of girls.

For decades, the problem of boys' educational underachievement in industrialized countries remained a hidden problem. It was generally accepted that girls outperformed boys in language and humanities subjects, but as long as boys achieved better results in mathematics and science it was assumed that there was an overall balance.

In recent years, however, girls' participation and performance in science and mathematics have significantly improved, due not just to school-based initiatives but also to wider changes in social expectations of women's roles. Boys' performance in language-based subjects has, however, not improved, with the result that girls have a better record across the board, as reflected in national tests from primary level through to public examinations at the end of school.

This has prompted substantial concern at government level. In Australia, for example, the Parliamentary Education Committee held an extensive inquiry into boys' education that made 24 recommendations ranging from classroom level through to educational and social policy.

The recommendations included promoting strategies that teachers can use to effectively engage all boys and girls, and making the issue of gender and achievement part of preservice and in-service teacher education.

In the United Kingdom, the Government has, since 1998, required all local education authorities to produce long-term strategies to counteract boys' underachievement, and for their progress to be regularly evaluated.The Government commissioned a three-year research project to identify successful strategies for raising boys' achievement without detriment to girls' and maintains a website dedicated to providing case studies, resources and guidance for schools on how to set up a strategy to tackle underachievement by boys.

A growing number of studies is deepening our understanding of boys' educational underachievement. Researchers have different areas of emphasis but all would broadly agree with the Australian Parliament's report that the phenomenon is complex and has a range of causes. It is clear that school-based remedies will be insufficient on their own and that the problem, like that of girls' underachievement in the developing world, is inseparable from wider questions about gender and power.

One suggestion has been that girls' socialization in the home encourages them to concentrate and stay 'on task', meaning that they are more amenable to the classroom environment. Research from Jamaica, for example, where girls outperform boys at secondary and tertiary levels, suggests that boys there are generally allowed a significant degree of freedom outside their homes while girls are expected to stay at home, required to spend their time on specific tasks.

A study by the Jamaican Government showed that gender differences in achievement can be attributed to a range of factors from socialization by parents in early childhood through to gender-biased messages in society as a whole, and also to the fact that boys and girls were treated differently in the classroom. Another potentially fruitful area for research and action connects schools with the wider question of social and sexual role-models: the gender balance of teachers.

A key strategy in sub-Saharan Africa to make schools more attractive and appropriate for girls is to increase the proportion of women teachers in a region in which the profession is dominated by men. The reverse may be true in industrialized countries and in Latin America and the Caribbean where, particularly at primary level, women teachers form the vast majority, leaving a potential absence of positive role models for young boys. Some researchers argue that one reason boys underperform so markedly in language and literature is that these are seen as 'girls' territory' and that reading is too often seen as 'unmanly'.

Boys' disaffection with education may be closely connected with their traditional socialization as males. It underlines the importance of fathers being involved with their children from birth, participating in their care and development during early childhood and supporting their education. Schools and education systems, though, inevitably have to cope with boys who have experienced no such positive example within their own families, and who respond instead to society's negative messages that encourage violence and behaviour that puts them and girls at risk.

In Nigeria, the Conscientizing Male Adolescents programme has been working with teenage boys since

1995. The programme involves schoolboys committing to a year of weekly discussions with a specially trained teacher in which they talk about gender roles and how they play out in their own families, in a society where rape and violence against women are areas of concern.

The curriculum is continually developing. A few years ago, it became evident that the boys were having trouble distinguishing love from sexual desire, so a curriculum unit was added on 'men's responsibility in sexual relationships, love and marriage'. The programme has found that it is important to find ways of addressing the idea of masculinity that are not too abstract – by discussing, for example, how boys feel when they don't do well in sports, or when they are pressured by male peers to chase girls or to be 'macho'. It is inevitably somewhat self-selecting, since boys have to be sufficiently motivated in the first place to enrol in the discussion groups.

Nevertheless, in its first 6 years 2,000 boys and young men graduated from the programme in the cities of Calabar and Uyo, and in 2002 more than 700 boys were enrolled. Boys who have graduated have gained significant skills in discussion and self-expression, which mark them out as 'stars', meaning that they are also likely to be seen as role models by others.

Boys can themselves be empowered and their own social and educational development extended by participating in attempts to protect and promote girls' rights. This has been evident in Uganda, where the Girls' Education Movement has, from its inception, involved boys as strategic allies. Girls in Kibale and Mbarara districts, for instance, established their local clubs and chapters in partnership with boys, working together to identify out-of-school children by name and location and then seeking them out.

Boys have been particularly valuable in addressing girls' security and safety issues during the commute to and from school – and also while they are in school. Given that the violence girls face comes from boys as well as men, the recruitment of boys as active allies in combating the problem has clear advantages for girls. But there is also an undeniable benefit to boys' own social development in their confronting violence and understanding why it is unacceptable. In Pakistan, too, adolescent boys are active and effective partners in promoting the rights of girls and women.

A project aimed at empowering adolescent girls has been running for over 6 years, and has reached 25,000 girls in 500 locations across Pakistan. The project met with significant success in providing knowledge, skills and new opportunities for girls. But over time the girls who were benefiting from the project made it known that they felt boys in their communities were starting to lag behind and recommended that the project be opened up to allow boys' participation.

In response, the training package for girls was modified appropriately for boys, and leaders were identified at each location whose skills were then developed, enabling them to guide follow-up activities and report progress. The object of including boys was to provide them with knowledge that would not only empower them but also help them acknowledge their new roles and enable them to understand and support girls' rights. The initiative was successfully piloted before being rolled out to 45 locations across all 4 provinces of the country. The initial response from the boys involved is encouraging. They have become more supportive of girls and have begun to get involved in constructive communitydevelopment activities.

In the Caribbean, governments have become increasingly aware that boys and young men are more likely to be alienated from school if they come from poor socioeconomic circumstances. There have been some interventions aimed specifically at such young males, such as the Youth Empowerment and Skills Training programme in the Bahamas, which targets those having trouble with the curriculum, and the Uplifting Adolescents Project in Jamaica, which focuses on the young unemployed outside the school system.

In Brazil, too, boys' problems with education are difficult to disentangle from their social class. Anderson's vivid picture of the call of the streets is backed up by a recent International Labour Organization study that looks at what it means to be in a Brazilian youth gang, a comando. In this kind of peer group a premium is put on actions and behaviours that are not likely to fit very easily into the average classroom, particularly in lowincome areas.

In addition, analysis of income data indicates that boys from poorer areas would have justification in thinking that schooling may not reap them sufficient financial rewards. People from low-income areas need to have 11 years of education before they reach the average earnings of people with just four years of schooling in metropolitan Rio de Janeiro as a whole.

In summary, the 'reverse gender gap' in Latin America and the Caribbean is by no means a simple phenomenon but rather one in which factors related to gender interact with class and race in telling ways, not to mention the individual differences, which of course mean that many boys perform well and happily in school while many girls find it extremely difficult.

The challenge for educational researchers and policy makers in the region – and in the industrialized countries that are noting similar trends – is to find ways of countering boys' negative experience of education while not reinforcing gender stereotypes. Gender sensitivity means what it says: being clear about the needs of both girls and boys, and creating school systems, classrooms and societies in which all children flourish – the ultimate objective of Education For All.

Strategies for Enhancing Girls Education

Girls' education is a dream investment for any Head of Government prepared to look beyond the immediate and usual solutions to the problems of development. Far from depriving other social development sectors, financing girls' education adds value to their work. It eases the strain on the health-care system by reducing both child and maternal mortality, by keeping children healthier and by reducing the incidence of HIV/AIDS. It increases women's skills and productivity, thereby reducing poverty and strengthening the economy in the long term.

The intimate connection between girls' education and other areas of development means, for example, that a single expenditure on supplying safe water and sanitation to a school has a double benefit: improving community health and hygiene and attracting more girls to school. The cost is surmountable. Estimates of the additional cost of achieving the Millennium Development Goal for education – universal primary education completion by

2015 – range between $9.1 billion and $38 billion per year. Associated with the $38 billion estimated by the World Bank, most of which would be borne by developing countries themselves, is a $5 billion to $7 billion funding gap that would need to be filled by externai aid. Between now and 2015 it might mean an additional aid bill of around $60 billion. This is a considerable sum, but it is substantially less than the cost of largescale military operations for which, it seems, money can always be found.

The practical barriers are also surmountable. There is practically no problem in education that does not have a solution already tried and tested elsewhere. The benefits attached to girls' education are unarguable, and the strategies and specific measures that can make a difference are well known. They have been applied in projects and programmes all over the world.

Years of experience have resulted in a more sophisticated understanding of exactly what kind of girls' education initiative works and what kind does not. Evaluations in sub-Saharan Africa, for example, have shown that a gender approach cannot simply be grafted on to an existing education programme. Wherever this has been tried, the existing programme has proved impervious to change. Girls' education projects have to be designed as such from the start and have to be backed by commitments from both government and programme planners.

Girls' education programmes must have three clear goals:

— reducing the total number of girls out of school;

— improving the quality of education for girls and boys alike; and

— ensuring progress in learning achievement for all children.

Weaving together interventions that address access with those that address quality helps fulfil the need to find excluded and at-risk children, especially girls, get them into school and ensure that they stay, learn and achieve in a safe and productive environment. Such interventions help ensure that education systems deliver results efficiently for all children.

The case of Afghanistan shows what is possible when the international community is seriously committed to tackling a crisis. It dramatizes what can be done when multiple factors – children's hunger to learn, parents' dreams for their children, a national government's readiness to lead and the international community's willingness to help – come together. Starved of education throughout decades of conflict, particularly during the Taliban era, the hunger of Afghan families for their children's chance to emergo to school was overwhelming. UNICEF's role in equipping them with educational materials in emergency conditions was the largest such operation ever undertaken by the organization.

To get and keep girls in school, integrated strategies are required at all levels – family, community, local and national government. For too long, girls' lack of education has been seen as a private matter, an issue to be dealt with by individual families.

The challenge of education for every girl is a challenge to development in all its sectors:

— To the minister of education

— To the minister of finance, who must allocate a sufficient share of the budget to primary education and make schools affordable by abolishing fees and providing poor families with an adequate wage.

— To the minister of health, who must provide adequate health services, water and sanitation.

— To the minister of labour, who is bound to establish standards of protection for working children so they are not exploited and denied education.

— To the minister of justice, who is bound to make schools safe.

— To the minister of planning, who must enable local communities and parents to oversee the services they need for their children to survive and thrive.

The 65 million girls out of school globally will never commandeer the world's attention in the same way as a war. They will not be rescued by tanks rolling through the desert. Screaming headlines about their plight will not boost media ratings or the circulation of daily newspapers. Their lost potential will not show up in front page photos to prick the conscience of the comfortable.

But their plight is an emergency nonetheless. Governments, aid agencies and international institutions must take practical steps to rescue them with as much urgency as if all 65 million were stranded in the mountains above a war zone, with TV cameras rolling.

Together, leaders from all levels of society must:

1. *Include girls' education as an essential component of development efforts:* Core human rights principles must inform economic development and poverty-reduction

programmes, and the rights of girls must be explicitly protected. If governments, international financial institutions, and bilateral and multilateral aid organizations applied social justice principles to development programmes, the outcome would be better for all of society –especially its most marginalized members.

— Public services have to be protected when economic crisis hits or national policy changes so that girls' rights to education, health, food and security are not infringed.

— Equal opportunity is not enough. We must focus on 'equality of outcome', ensuring that all children, girls and boys alike, obtain the same high-quality education.

— The right of children and their families to participate in the decisions that affect their lives must be respected. Their opinions must be taken into account in public matters affecting them, such as budget allocations for education and related development decisions.

Girls must have equal opportunities and be equally prepared for the kind of meaningful participation that is vital to democratic governance.

2. *Create a national ethos for girls' education*: A national ethos of 'no girl out of school' must be created, so that communities are as scandalized and concerned about the girls kept at home and out of school as they are about the boys and girls more visibly exploited at work. Creating this ethos requires a widespread civiceducation campaign, explaining the benefits of girls' education to the family and to society. Every

sector of society must be brought on board, from politicians to parents, from the private sector to the mass media. Governments should be held accountable for getting and keeping girls in school. To this end:

— The number of out-of-school girls must be routinely and publicly reported – and considered a matter of national concern as urgent as rising unemployment rates.

— Countries should consider introducing an education tax or commodities surcharge to be used exclusively to get girls or boys into school until gender parity is achieved.

— Governments should do an inventory of successful projects in their countries, bring these to national scale, and audit their effectiveness in having girls complete a basic education.

3. *Allow no school fees of any kind:* School is not an optional add-on, to be funded if and when the economy improves – it is a human right. When education systems work on this principle they will go the extra mile to guarantee schooling to the most marginalized and disadvantaged, the majority of whom are most always girls. Primary school must be free, universal and compulsory, and parents must have a choice in the kind of education their children receive. All school fees and charges for primary school must be immediately abolished. When parents have to pay for their children's schooling, Education For All becomes impossible and girls lose out even more than boys. Education must be embraced as the right of every child.

4. *Think both outside and inside the 'education box':* Education in general – and girls' education in particular – must be completely integrated into each country's poverty reduction strategy or other relevant national plans for poverty reduction. Programmes that work must be scaled up.

   Girls' schooling can and should be promoted by actions such as:

   — Anti-discrimination laws and policies that protect girls and women

   — HIV/AIDS prevention programmes that focus on girls and women

   — Early childhood programmes that treat boys and girls equally and address the issue ofgender roles and relations

   — Investment in water and sanitation for homes and schools

   — Efforts to reduce violence in communities and protect children from exploitation and abuse, with special attention to the situation of girls. At the same time, investment in education should be based on the abundant evidence of the positive results in schools when there are:

   — Increased opportunities for girls' participation, including in sports, cultural activities, civic affairs and school government

   — Incentive packages and financial assistance for families who send and keep their girls in school, and actively contribute to improving their performance

— Teachers trained in child rights and gendersensitive classroom techniques

— Teachers receiving a regular, living wage

— Parents empowered in the management and support of schools; involving them in parentteacher associations; and giving them assistance to create a better learning environment in the home and to project a positive expectation of their children's achievement.

5. *Establish schools as centres of community development:* Schools and less-formal learning spaces should become more than places for lessons and skillbuilding; they should become centres of community participation and development. UNICEF's experience in conflict and emergency situations has shown education's power to transform tragedy and chaos into healing and hope, as it restores structure to young lives, rehabilitates their spirit, and offers understanding to children facing futures that are, at best, uncertain. Similarly, the HIV/AIDS pandemic brings home the lessons of education's role in an emergency. Schools have proven to be the most efficient and cost-effective means of protecting children and young people from HIV infection. This fact alone presents a strong case for schools as the centre of efforts to combat the spread of the disease and mitigate its impact. Just as schools must become flexible enough to meet the needs of all children, whether they are girls traditionally excluded from education or children living on the streets, they must also address the growing number of children orphaned and made vulnerable by HIV/AIDS. It is education that can

best empower children and young people – particularly orphans and girls most vulnerable to the disease – with the knowledge they need to protect themselves and their communities, and help them acquire the knowledge and skills needed to build a better future. And it is education that can unravel the discrimination and ignorance that perpetuate the spread of HIV/AIDS. Thus, education should become the centre of work around HIV/AIDS and other threats to the survival of children and young people.

6. *Integrate strategies:* Integrated strategies are required to confront the multifaceted barriers to girls' education. This should occur at three levels: investments, policies and institutions; service delivery; and in conceptual frameworks, namely those of the economic and human rights approaches.

   a. *Investment, policy and institutional initiatives:* It is not enough to allocate financial resources for certain goals without addressing policies that might hinder their effectiveness. Building more schools will have limited impact if user fees and other barriers continue to prevent enrolment. In the same way, available resources are most productive when the policy and institutional environment encourages their use. Decentralization, for example, as well as legal reforms, partnerships and participation all improve resource effectiveness.

   b. *Service delivery.* Effective coordination of services in education, health, nutrition, water and sanitation – especially in the delivery of such services – can improve programme effectiveness. At the community level, for example, a school committee can be the focal point for immunization, nutrition and sanitation interventions as well as for those services more directly related to education.

c. *Conceptual frameworks.* Generally, economic frameworks are used to prepare investment, policy or institutional tools. When these tools are based entirely on economic principles they prove ineffective in delivering programme objectives to the poorest and most marginalized individuals. However, when the economic approach is informed by human rights principles, programmes for poverty reduction, social development and disparity reduction become far more effective.

7. *Increase international funding for education:* All industrialized countries should direct 10 per cent of official aid to basic education, with programmes that benefit girls as their priority. They can achieve this by making good on their commitment made at the International Conference on Financing for Development in Monterrey, Mexico to move swiftly towards giving at least 0.7 per cent of gross national product in aid, and at least 0.15 per cent to the least developed countries.

Extend the Fast-Track Initiative to cover more countries and guarantee swift funding for their needs. All countries that have qualified for fasttrack help in their pursuit of Education For All must urgently receive the financial assistance they have been promised by donor governments. The Initiative should be expanded to include all governments that demonstrate a serious commitment to the goal of universal primary education.

Unless the world focuses its attention on the 2005 target date for girls' education, the Millennium Development Goals for 2015 are going to slide by, unrealized. Unless the international community acts now, another generation of girls will be lost to ignorance, abuse, exploitation and HIV/AIDS – and, in a future that is nearer than we would think, we will later lose millions of their young children to unnecessary deaths, avoidable malnutrition and disease and squandered human potential.

Girls' education is an arena in which we do not have to wait for science; we know very well what is needed and what works. The Millennium Development Goals are under threat; investing in girls' education will put us on track to meet them. Development is faltering; girls' education will give it new momentum.

Millions of children are affected by HIV/AIDS; gender-sensitive schools can become havens of care and comfort. The rights of children around the world are abused daily and systematically; ensuring the rights of girls to an education is the bridge to safety and protection for all children.

Strategies Inside the Classroom

The strategies that follow, whether working from inside or outside the classroom, have been proven to increase school attendance and completion by girls. Each promotes in its own way the model of a school that seeks to ensure effective learning in safe, healthy gendersensitive and child-centred environments.

No country could implement all of these strategies at once. Governments should undertake an analysis of the particular barriers facing girls as a necessary prelude to selecting a package of the most pertinent interventions. An opinion poll of the perceptions of parents and children of those barriers would play an important part in such an analysis.

Making education free and compulsory is the keystone of any national plan to eliminate gender disparity in education and achieve universal education. Faced with an economically driven choice between sending sons or daughters to school, poor families often send their sons.

Removing fees or offering financial support to families with daughters in school, as well as explaining the advantages of sending girls to school, can make a real difference. In Malawi, for example, the initial result of abolishing school fees in 1994 was an increase in enrolment of almost 70 per cent, from 1.9 million in the 1993/94 academic year to 3.2 million in the 1994/95 academic year.Strategies within the classroom

Making the classroom more child-centred and gender-sensitive, and rooted in the life and environment of the community. The Nueva Escuela Unitaria Bilingüe intercultural programme in Guatemala is founded on participatory teaching and learning, with play and study creatively combined. Teachers make full use of Mayan languages and culture that have in the past been marginalized despite their importance to half the country's population. The result is a completion rate above the national average and a high enrolment rate for girls.

Recruiting and training teachers who are sensitive to gender and child rights, and paying them a regular, living wage. Both female and male teachers should receive training in gender awareness in the classroom. Without this, some countries, such as Zambia, found that teachers may value and encourage boys' participation in class more than they value girls' and may allocate school tasks along strict gender lines, leaving girls to sweep the floors or clean the toilets.

While one cannot assume that all women teachers are gender-sensitive in their teaching methods, there is a specific need in some areas to recruit more women teachers who can serve as role models for girls and may make girls' parents feel more comfortable. Countries that achieve higher enrolment in primary education tend to employ a high proportion of female teachers.

In Kenya, the Strengthening Primary School Management project, funded by the United Kingdom Department for International Development, requires one of every two head teachers or principals receiving training to be a woman. As a consequence, the proportion of women head teachers was boosted from 10 per cent to 23 per cent over a 10-year period, and female teachers at primary school level account for 41 per cent of the total. The primary school completion rate also improved over the same time: the completion rate for 1994 to 2001 was 46 per cent (boys 48 per cent and girls 43 per cent). The rate improved in 2002 to 56 per cent for both boys and girls. The percentage of trained primary school teachers has increased from 70 per cent in 1990 to 97 per cent in 2002.

Promoting Health

In Myanmar, one programme adopts a holistic, life skills approach to health. The School-Based Healthy Living and HIV/AIDS Prevention Education programme is taught as part of the standard curriculum to children from grades 2 to 9. It focuses on a range of health and social issues – from HIV/AIDS to personal hygiene, from nutrition to drugs – and explores them through activities designed to develop life skills such as communication, cooperation and problem-solving.

The programme has led to dramatic success stories, such as a village in Tachileik township that started using iodized salt as a result of pressure from children who had learned of its benefits in one such class. Introduced in 1998, the programme now covers 1.3 million students in nearly 9,000 schools and is being adopted by the Government as the standard for life skills teaching throughout Myanmar.

Promoting Sports

Providing girls with access to sport can also contribute to achieving gender parity in education. With sports in many countries a traditionally male domain, girls' participation challenges gender stereotypes, breaking down entrenched attitudes. As female athletes gain recognition, they become mentors to others. Through sports, girls are given the chance to be leaders and improve their confidence and self-esteem.

As girls participate in sports, they acquire new interpersonal skills and through additional social networks gain access to different opportunities, allowing them to become more engaged in school and community life. In Romania, sport has increased school participation among the minority Roma community by providing an opportunity for girls and boys to participate in teams, conditional to school attendance and academic performance.

In Zimbabwe, the Youth Education through Sport programme, led by young people, requires participants to commit themselves to staying in school and to volunteering in their communities. The programme's aim is for them to adopt life skills, become peer educators and contribute to their communities as positive role models. Since 2000, the programme has reached 25,000 young people in 10 provinces.

Eliminating Gender Bias from Learning Tools

Apart from the obvious value to girls, the thoughtful revision of textbooks, classroom materials and lesson plans is likely to increase their quality and relevance to the lives of all children. In Viet Nam, the Government is developing new gendersensitive teacher-training modules, ensuring that future textbooks are gender neutral, and providing training in gender and child rights to national education managers and members of local parent-teacher associations. In Somalia, a gender-based approach to curricula development and teacher training has increased enrolment by 28 per cent to more than 260,000 (although the percentage of girls remained stationary at 35 per cent). There is now a higher demand for education by parents and communities, and increased numbers of women are becoming active members of community education committees.

Scheduling Flexibly of Lessons

Children are often excluded from school because of family responsibilities or the homework that is more often allocated to girls than boys. BRAC schools in Bangladesh have given priority to girls and inspired many other countries to follow their example. The school schedule is flexible; though it runs for two hours a day, six days a week, the times are set by local parents, and the school calendar is adapted to fit local considerations such as the harvest.

BRAC schools met with such success that the scheme expanded quickly, and total enrolment is now at about 1.2 million. As a result of the programme's special emphasis on girls' enrolment, about 70 per cent of children in non-formal primary education and schools providing basic education for older children are female. Around 97 per cent of the teachers in BRAC schools are women.

Usage of Local Language

When the language of instruction is different from the children's mother tongue, it is often more disabling for girls, who tend to be less exposed to social environments beyond their immediate families.In Peru, girls and boys are first taught in Quechua, their mother tongue, and subsequently learn Spanish as a second language.

The proposal for Intercultural Bilingual Education to be applied to multigrade classrooms and oneteacher schools for native Quechua speakers in poor rural Andean areas has contributed to a 50 per cent increase in writing and communication abilities for girls and boys. In Burundi, studies show that after mothertongue instruction was introduced in 1973, the effect was to greatly increase access to school, leading to higher attendance overall. To meet the consequent high demand on schooling, the special measure of double shifting was introduced.

Strategies Outside the Classroom

Gathering gender-specific education statistics, including those on learning achievement at primary, secondary and tertiary levels. All countries now gather statistics measuring enrolment of girls and boys. This data is vital if the quality of teaching and learning is to be improved and progress towards the Millennium Development Goals is to be measured.

In addition to gender, wherever feasible, data should be disaggregated by factors including urban or rural location, household wealth and mothers' education. Analysis of such data is invaluable in showing disparities within disparities, for example, how gender intertwines with poverty or ethnicity to produce multiple disadvantages. Few countries, however, monitor learning achievement in a sufficiently systematic way, and still fewer break their results down by gender.

Providing Early Childhood Programmes

All children are likely to benefit from pre-school care, but evidence suggests that it enhances girls' preparedness for school more than boys'. What is more, it is the first point, after the family, at which gender stereotypes can be addressed. In Bolivia, the Kallpa Wawa and Khuskamanta Wiñaspa programmes combine literacy training for adult women with early childhood care. Indigenous Quechua women are taught to read and write as they learn about child care, nutrition, health, education and protection.

As a result of the programme, almost 5,000 children have been registered and provided with a birth certificate, more than 11,000 Quechua families have been trained in integrated child development; and some 1,500 indigenous women have been trained and now work as child development promoters in 22 municipalities with high poverty indices.

Enabling Young Mothers to Return to Schools

In many countries girls who become pregnant while at school are forbidden to return to their studies. The Forum for African Women Educationalists has been particularly active in lobbying governments in sub-Saharan Africa to change this policy. In Zambia, a 1997 policy allows re-admitting schoolgirls after they give birth, yet very few girls return due to perceived stigma and bullying from their peers. In Chile, the Ministry of Education in 1990 instructed schools not to expel any pregnant girl. However, the ruling proved difficult to enforce, and the Government submitted to Parliament a law, approved in 2000, guaranteeing the right of girls to continue and complete their education, while demanding from schools the necessary academic facilities.

Taking Special Measures for the Disadvantaged

In some countries and regions where ethnic minorities, people living in rural areas and the poor face discrimination and exclusion, girls often suffer a multiple disadvantage because of their gender. The more disadvantaged the girl, the more essential it is that the education system should reach out to her through special measures, rather than just assuming she will be drawn in as part of a general drive for education for all.

In Bhutan, 80 per cent of the population live by subsistence farming, scattered over mountain slopes rather than clustered in towns. Some 261 community schools have been established in huts, temples or farmhouses rather than in specialized school buildings, with management and supervision vested in parents and the local community. Since the schools belong to the community, they create a sense of ownership, and so are better maintained, and parents show more interest in education.

The Department of Education has successfully narrowed the difference in the proportion of primary school enrolment between boys and girls from 24 per cent in 1990 (girls 38 per cent, boys 62 per cent) to 6 per cent in 2000 (girls 47 per cent, boys 53 per cent). The drop-out rate has decreased from 8 per cent in 1995 to 4 per cent in 1999 for both girls and boys.

Providing Alternative Education for Girls

One way of reaching girls who have dropped out of school, as well as other groups such as working children and children in conflict situations, is through education centres established outside the formal school system.

In Turkey, learning centres in five provinces encourage girls normally confined to the home and domestic labour, to enrol in 'open primary school'. The centres perform an invaluable social as well as educational function; girls have organized field trips to neighbouring provinces and even drama clubs involving local boys. The Turkish Ministry of Education has adopted the open primary school as a model for its own girls' education strategy.

Providing Alternative Education for Overaged Children

In the United Republic of Tanzània, the Complementary Basic Education in Tanzania programme serves an estimated 3 million over age children and adolescents who are out of school. It provides basic education through a specially designed threeyear course, at the end of which children are eligible to join the mainstream school system.

Girls were the initial focus of the project due to their low enrolment rates. But the difficulty in locating them, either because they were working indoors or they married, failed to adequately address gender in the enrolment process. It has been successful in reaching excluded or 'hidden' groups of children, including orphans, children of single parents and young mothers. The project has been mainstreamed into the formal education system to cater to all over age children and adolescents who will not be eligible to enter the school system under new rules that stipulate age as a condition for entry.

Locating schools closer to children's homes, if necessary by establishing small, multigrade or multiage schools in remote rural areas. Girls are less likely to be able to make a long journey from home to school, not least because of concerns about their safety en route.Burkina Faso, for example, has developed a network of 'satellite schools'. These are small schools that accommodate only the first three grades, allowing the youngest children (who start school at the age of 7) to gain their first experience of school in or close to their own villages. Since their establishment in 1995, 229 satellite schools have reached over 100,000 girls and boys.

Compared with pupils in the conventional school system, children who graduate from satellite schools perform at a higher level in all subjects including reading, writing and mathematics, with performance rates one-and-a half to two times as high. Satellite schools also have a remarkable retention rate of almost 95 per cent. These positive results can be explained by a number of factors including the use of local language that makes learning quicker; parental engagement; and a lower average student-to-teacher ratio of 29 to 1 in satellite schools compared with 48 to 1 in conventional schools.

Making Sure Safety

This involves making schools secure not only from without – perimeter walls have, for example, been found to increase girls' sense of safety in many countries – but also from within. Education is a key to protection when it is of good quality, but falls short when the learning environment itself fails to provide the necessary protection against violence and abuse of children.

When schools are associated with sexual or physical gender violence, girls' access to education is negatively affected. Parents will naturally hesitate to send their daughters to schools that are thought to be sites of physical or sexual gender violence.

Boys and girls are often susceptible to psychological and physical violence in different ways, and adolescents in particular can find themselves especially vulnerable to violations of their safety. Lack of safety and security in the school environment may be very obvious in terms of physical danger, such as beatings or rape. The abuse of girls – sexual, physical and emotional by teachers is a common problem.

Breaking the silence about violence at school is an important step towards its diagnosis and prevention. The Gambia did this by including in a sexual harassment policy a directive stating that teachers should not be alone with pupils of the opposite sex.

The launch of a two-year UN Global Study on Violence, the recommendations of the Commission on Human Security, the momentum behind the Millennium Development Goals and the ongoing Education For All movement all offer opportunities for substantive empirical research and advocacy around safety in education.

Encouraging Girls' Participation

Girls can be the most effective and inspiring advocates of child-friendly education if they are given the chance. The Girls' Education Movement is a dynamic pan- African girls' organization supported by the Forum for African Woman Educationalists as well as by the Governments of Norway and Uganda.

Launched in 2001, the Movement aims not just to galvanize action for education for all, but also to change the character of school systems so that "they offer rich, rewarding and friendly learning experiences for all children." Through the process of school mapping and the use of indigenous knowledge, the clubs were able to identify homes with out-of-school children, develop a list of all the children who were not going to school within the school's catchment area and take the initiative in bringing them to school.

As a result, not only has girls' enrolment increased, but there has also been a shift in the way girls are perceived, from passive victims to active, vocal and engaged participants. The Movement has made a point of involving boys as active advocates of gender-sensitive Education For All.

Involving the Local Community

The Community Empowerment Project in Jordan led to the village of Al-Rashedieh holding a community meeting, where women discussed their worries about their daughters being forced to stop school due to the absence of a secondary school for girls in the area. The women prepared a petition and went to plead their case with the director of the education ministry in Aqaba. Within six months, three fully equipped girls' secondary classes had been established.

The Opening Doors for Girls' Education project in the rural Andean areas of Peru, which have been affected by extreme poverty and conflicts over the past two decades, involves 324,000 inhabitants of 540 communities in monitoring girls' inclusion in society and their right to a good education. This participatory monitoring strategy has benefited more than 65,000 girls. In Sudan, the Child-Friendly Community Project shows how community involvement made a difference in the number of girls in school and the quality of education for girls and boys alike.

Supplying Good Sanitation Facilities

Many girls drop out of school at the onset of menstruation, partly because there are no separate toilet facilities. Sometimes it is not enough simply to provide the latrines, however. Girls' involvement in identifying their location and type can be critical in determining whether they will be used. UNICEF has helped provide 1,400 schools in Pakistan with water and sanitation and is currently promoting school sanitation and hygiene in 46 other countries.

Decreasing the Domestic Workload

Many girls are kept at home to help with domestic tasks. Supplying communities or women's groups with equipment such as mills to grind cereals, huskers, carts and plastic barrels for water conservation, can decrease the amount of work to be done so that girls can be freed to attend school. Girls may also be prevented from going to school because they have to fetch water from a traditional well or remote water pump. Creating water points can alleviate their workload, as well as provide safe water for the whole community. Day-care community centres for children under six can relieve girls from looking after their siblings, thereby allowing them to go to school.

Involving General Public

The rights and well-being of children are best served when relations between men and women in the household are based on mutual respect, equal rights and shared responsibilities. Men often can play unique and positive roles in the lives of children and often actively support efforts to reduce gender inequality.

National Efforts

The most successful girls' education initiatives incorporate many or most of these facets into an integrated programme. Zambia's Programme for the Advancement of Girls' Education is a case in point. Its 12 'interactive interventions' have been so successful that what was a pilot project in the mid-1990s has now been extended all over the country. Piloted in 1995 in 20 schools, the programme was operational in over 1,000 schools in all 72 districts by 2002.

Another example of a national effort on behalf of children's right to education is the Sarva Shiksha Abhiyan, launched in October 2001. It is the Government of India's policy statement in universal elementary education that provides a framework from which to reach out to all children in the 6 to 14 year old age group by 2010. It seeks primarily to promote community-owned, quality education. It recognizes that education at this level should be made useful and relevant by improving the curriculum, focusing on child-centred activities, effective and innovative teaching aids and strategies and training teachers to further the quality agenda. For instance, the State of Kerala undertook a study on classroom processes with a gender focus in 168 schools in order to develop a teacher-training module. Almost 28,000 teachers received the training and reference material to help them transform their classrooms.

The initiative seeks particularly to bridge social, regional and gender gaps by targeting children of socially vulnerable and economically marginal groups – girls, scheduled caste and scheduled tribe children and children belonging to minority groups – with the active participation of the community in the management of schools. It has provision for the distribution of free textbooks to all girls and children belonging to the scheduled caste and scheduled tribes up to grade 8. It provides for interventions in early childhood care and education, indirectly helping to ease the burden of sibling care on girls.

The strategies advocated and implemented by the Sarva Shiksha Abhiyan are embedded in community ownership of school-based interventions through the effective decentralization and involvement of various institutions. It is seen as a partnership between the central, state and local governments while providing states with an opportunity to individually develop their own vision of elementary education. This process involves the creation and support of local bodies like the Mother Teacher Associations and Parent Teacher Associations and bringing them together with the Panchayati Raj Institutions, school management committees, village education committees and others in the management of elementary schools.

4

Changing Trends of School Facilities

Schools across the world are under increasing pressure to do better. Developed countries track student achievement data closely, offering rewards and imposing sanctions for changes in performance over time. While devloping countries require high school students to pass statewide tests in order to graduate. It is self-evident that such systems create pressure for performance. In USA, the recently enacted federal elementary and secondary education package calls for even more tests and accountability, makes it clear that standards-based reforms are fast becoming "a fundamental part" of education policy and governance in America.

While attention to disparities in educational access peaked during the civil rights movement, school systems around the world are showing a renewed focus on the gap in achievement between poor and minority students and their middle-class white counterparts. In some cities, parents and community activists have organized marches and rallies pressing school leaders to improve schools that serve poor and minority students. Districts and states are beginning to respond by giving failing schools, sometimes called 'focus schools' or 'target schools,' extra support and/or some other intervention.

Add to this the roll back of affirmative action in college admissions, the general focus on test scores, and the increasing ethnic and linguistic diversity in the nation's classrooms, and it is clear why pressure for increased minority achievement is at the forefront of discussions about the future of learning in America. For many years, a family's choices about where to send their children to school were relatively simple: attend a neighborhood public school, or pay tuition at a local private or religious school.

By contrast, today's choices are complicated. For starters, "choice" can mean many different things: it can mean parents are able to choose where their child goes to school within a school district; or, it can mean choice between districts; it can mean the presence of charter schools; or, it can mean giving parents vouchers to attend privately run schools.

School choice can even mean allowing home schooling parents to enroll their children part-time in district-run classes, sports, and art programs. All of these "choices" are evident nationwide, though some are more widely available than others. Though the evidence varies, it is clear that, in some districts, competitive choice has an effect on traditional public schools, leading them to try new ways to attract students and to boost achievement.

To the degree that choice in any of these forms forces schools to compete for students, it may add to the pressure on all schools to perform. Research shows that the achievement gap grows more slowly in small schools and that small schools generally boost minority achievement.

As such, performance pressure, especially performance pressure associated with the achievement gap, may lead to smaller schools or other new classroom configurations.

When schools are held accountable for performance, principals may demand more control over school resources. A bottom-up organization would allow principals to make programme and resource decisions that fit their school's unique needs. Ultimately, if performance pressure is coupled with sanctions and rewards, the logic of standards-based reform raises the possibility that the supply of schools will change. Successful schools will prosper; struggling schools will ultimately change or close.

In response to standards-based reform and new graduation requirements, (e.g., a certificate of mastery), parents with choices - or districts under accountability pressure - may demand new grade spans in schools. For example, some schools might focus on the transition years between junior high and high school only; others might focus on the final years of high school.

None of these changes is certain to occur. But they represent likely responses to pressures that are certain to come. Recent research on small high schools has highlighted the fact that some students are more successful in schools that, thanks to their size, can pay close attention to their students' individual needs. In particular, it appears that some students from minority backgrounds can do better in small schools

The demand for personalized programs may lead to more off-campus activity for older students. Schools that offer quality school-to-work programs, for example, might provide a "work-based education coordinated with school-based instruction". As high schools try to meet their students' needs, they may make greater use of off campus resources at community colleges. Students may attend advanced placement and other courses at a community college, gaining access to more choices and benefiting from a seamless continuum of education from high school to college.

The middle college high school model (wherein students attend school on a community college campus, taking both high school and college courses) provides another example of possible links between high school and college.

Role of New Technologies

Technology's importance in the future of education is a given. After all, 9 in 10 school age children have access to computers and the Internet is now "pervasive". But technology's importance in education is not only due to its sheer presence. It is also driven by:

— The demand for technology savvy graduates

— The demand for technology-based solutions to teacher/skill shortages

— Demand for technology savvy graduates.

Rapid technological change is the seminal force in the economy. Looking ahead 20 years, forecasters predict that new technologies will continue to increase the demand for tech savvy workers, creating "new jobs [that] pay better and require higher skills" than jobs lost in the process. Public schools will be under increasing pressure to ensure that their graduates are prepared for these jobs.

Demand for technology-based solutions to teacher/ skill shortages. As the nascent online education industry develops, schools that face skill or teacher shortages will be able to access relevant instructional programs through the Internet or other interactive media. As these and other online educational services become increasingly relevant and high quality, they may offer schools new tools for reaching students, especially those who may not be learning well through more traditional approaches.

And so, What will the demand for and availability of new technology mean for schools? For starters, it may lead to:

— New mixes of teachers and computers. Apex Learning, K-12 Inc., Cyber School, and other online education providers allow schools to use an array of teacher-computer combinations. Accordingly, schools may need spaces that serve a variety of class sizes depending on whether instruction is computer-based or teacher-based.

— Students learning off campus. Just as school-to-work connections will move students out of the classroom and into the community, computer coursework and distance learning create an opportunity for students to learn at home or at their local library as well as at school.

— Movable walls and wiring flexibility. As technologies change, schools will need to be able to adapt their spaces to take full advantage of technological innovations.

Today, teacher shortages are concentrated in urban districts and in certain subject areas, namely math, science, and special education. But districts everywhere urban, suburban, and rural - fear a potential shortage of teachers (and principals) that will bring significant challenges in the coming decades. The reasons behind teacher shortages are complex, and they may vary from region to region. But on a very basic level, there is a microeconomic story behind the shortages that can be summed up by two factors:

— Increases in the demand for teachers

— Stagnation in the supply of teachers

The demand for teachers has been growing over time, in part because of expanding enrollments and class size reduction policies. According to current projections, these patterns show no sign of changing in the coming decade. In addition, the need for new teachers is caused in part by teacher departures. Some leave out of frustration with their work environment, others leave to pursue different professional opportunities, still others leave for personal reasons (e.g., the birth of children or a spouse relocation).

Some school may seek new configurations with regards to administration, counselling/mentoring, and classroom teaching. Leadership and management functions may become more diffuse and entrepreneurial as principals do things like mixing full- time teachers with part-timers or Internet coursework as they look for new learning opportunities for students.

As a particular school site faces human resource constraints, it may draw on other schools or nearby community colleges and other organizations to supplement its program and teaching force. Because fluctuations in numbers of students, their location, and their socio economic status impact demands on schools, districts pay close attention to demographic forecasts and trends.

In US, on a national level, K-12 enrolment is slated to continue to expand to a record 53.4 million by 2005 and then to decline to 53 million by 2011. Most of this growth will be in the western states. While enrolment drops and rises will inevitably continue, demographic shifts will take on new importance as students enrolled in the nation's schools becomes increasingly diverse. Since the Civil Rights era, for example, the number of Black and Hispanic students in USA has grown by 5.8 million while the number of white students has shrunk by 5.6 million.

Today the United States has the most diverse student population in its history, and in the coming decades this trend will only increase. What will these fluctuations and shifts in demo-graphics mean for schools? For starters, it may lead to:

— An over or undersupply of school buildings. Within a relatively short period of time a district may face an overall influx of students or it may face a long drain of school-aged children. Even within a district some parts of town may have overflowing enrolment while others may be under enrolled.

— Trade-offs between transportation and facilities. As districts face an imbalance of facilities and enrolment, they will want to make strategic decisions about whether or not to invest in transportation (moving students to where the buildings are) or in facilities.

— Demand for new approaches to teaching students from diverse backgrounds. Schools with large populations of students learning English as a second language, for example, may want to develop the most effective approaches to meeting the needs of those children.

These five trends could have a profound or limited impact on a school district. Exactly what any city's schools like in 10, 20, or 25 years will depend on a complicated interplay between national trends and state, district, and neighbourhood factors.

Building Facilities

Taken together, the five national trends - performance pressure, demands for personalization, new technologies, and changes in teacher and student populations - have serious implications for the future of school facilities. Above all, they imply a host of new classroom and school configurations. These trends may drive large schools, particularly high schools, to break themselves into several smaller independent units, while sharing one large existing building. They may drive other schools to be built with moveable walls and wiring to accommodate changing school needs and technological innovations (much like current commercial space in urban areas).

At the farthest extreme, other schools may be "virtual schools," engaging students in on-line learning accessed at home, in local libraries, or in special labs designed and built for these purposes. Indeed, some students in the future may spend only two or three days a week at a dedicated school building. The rest of the week they may be engaged in off-campus internships, service learning projects, or field research.

As more and more off-campus learning opportunities are demanded and developed, one can imagine some high schools that look less like a comprehensive center for all student learning and activity, and more like a home base from which students launch their individually tailored learning plans.

Some school districts, overwhelmed by this complexity, may be tempted to disregard all but the most traditional and readily achievable space arrangements. But in doing so they may limit the educational options available to students in their charge. In the end, traditional (and often formulaic) plans for school facilities will not do. To make sense of these changes, districts will need a strategic approach to facilities provision. This means that in addition to outlining steps to accomplish over a specific time period, they will need to develop criteria or principles that guide their decisions about school space. The following six criteria, based on the five trends and their implications for school spaces, offer an example:

1. Facilities should focus on student learning and achievement
2. Facilities should be flexible
3. Facilities should be responsive
4. Facilities trade-offs and choices should be transparent
5. Facilities provision should be driven by data
6. Facilities should be economically efficient

Focused on Student Learning and Achievement

Ideas about student learning and achievement should drive decisions about school space, rather than the other way around. School leaders, parents and students who have promising ideas for increasing student learning should be encouraged to dream about the ideal school space they need to achieve their goals. Of course, practical considerations and trade-offs have to be considered, but the district need not allow those issues to become excuses for not finding or creating school spaces that will enhance teaching and learning.

Flexible

Above all, the future requires flexible facilities - flexible in design, usage, and financing. Performance pressures, personalization, technology, changes in teacher supply, and demographic shifts all have the potential to drive new methods of instruction and assessment. Many of these same factors will push for new school and classroom configurations. Accordingly, a school facilities plan for the future must be agile enough to find and provide schools with a variety of spaces. It must also be able to reclaim space and redistribute it when needed.

Responsive

This criterion is closely related to the last. If performance pressure drives schools to demand more autonomy, administrators and teachers must be involved in discussions and decisions about their buildings and space. In short, in the future, facilities supply needs to be more than just flexible; it also needs to be responsive to principals and teachers' needs and suggestions about the spaces in which they work. It must be both "bottom up" and "top down."

Transparent

This criterion follows from the last two. If facilities supply is to be flexible and responsive, it is vital that it is credible too -principals and teachers have to have the sense that the process for making facilities decisions is fair. If costs and the rationale behind decisions are unclear, end users may see space administration and facilities decisions as capricious and inevitably come away disappointed or angry. The only way to assure confidence in the process is to conduct it in an open and public manner.

Driven by Data

In order to be flexible, responsive, and open, a facilities plan for the future needs good information. Districts need information about the spaces they own (or those they have access to), including data about their location, what condition they are in, and who is using them and for how long. Accordingly, a school district or other agency responsible for matching schools with facilities should conduct yearly audits of all available space.

In addition to some computerized inventory, a facilities plan for the future needs accurate demographic information about enrollment trends as well as information from policymakers about program and policy decisions that are on the horizon. System administrators must use this information to plan comprehensively and proactively, not incrementally and reactively. In the end, all facility projects need to be justified by data that is consistently gathered about structures, people, and programs.

Efficient

Despite its somewhat distasteful connotation among educators, efficiency is an important criterion for school facilities. In education, efficiency means focusing spending on productive activity, i.e. instruction. Through innovative partnerships or other arrangements, districts may be able to redirect resources away from inefficient facilities and toward instruction.

Districts should also ask themselves if the potential exists for improving the quality of facilities without increasing public spending, or if it is possible to provide the same quality of facilities at a lesser cost to taxpayers. Today is an especially ripe time for districts to consider rethinking their school buildings along these lines. This is because, in addition to the five national trends already outlined, districts across USA face a pressing need to add, renovate or replace aging educational facilities.

By thinking strategically, districts have an opportunity for having their goals, priorities and strategies for raising student achievement drive their facilities decisions. Rather than allowing practical constraints and a desire to satisfy all constituents determine their choices, school districts can think about trends in education both national and local - as they plan for the future.

In the Portland Public Schools and the Niagara Falls City School District, ideas about instruction and learning are driving the provision, design, and use of school buildings. Portland's facilities strategy was built on several years' worth of work already underway in the district. Portland identified two major trends that it believes will shape the future of its public schools. First, the district realizes that it has and will continue to have a decreasing school-age population. According to the projections of the Population Center at Portland State University, in ten years the city will serve 4,500 fewer students than it does now. Second, the district anticipates that changing practices in teaching and learning will require new kinds of school buildings. In addition, Portland decided that environmentally sound facilities management was important for the future health of the city.

The Portland Schools Real Estate Trust is a new independent non-profit that will act as the district's professional "real estate assistant." In the beginning, the district envisions the Trust helping it negotiate leases, sales, and purchases of property. In the longer run, the Trust might take on more responsibility for managing the district's real estate. According to the plan, the Trust will work with three key purposes in mind:

1) to generate annual net revenue for the district
2) to help the district meet its goal of flexible property management and
3) to allow the district to focus its energies on its core mission, education, instead of "technical and community issues related to real estate".

Portland has realized that it cannot do everything it wants to do and hope to do it well. If it has too many competing purposes, some will inevitably get neglected. In addition, school officials, like other public officials facing elections, have an incentive to focus on the here and now - on operating expenses - and tend to neglect long-term capital investment needs.

School Feeding Programmes

Health and nutritional status are powerful influences on a child's learning and on how well a child performs in school. Children who lack certain nutrients in their diet (particularly iron and iodine), or who suffer from protein-energy malnutrition, hunger, parasitic infections or other diseases, do not have the same potential for learning as healthy and well-nourished children. Weak health and poor nutrition among school-age children diminish their cognitive development either through physiological changes or by reducing their ability to participate in learning experiences - or both.

Contrary to conventional wisdom, nutritional status does not improve with age. The extra demands on school-age children (to perform chores, for example, or walk long distances to school) create a need for energy that is much greater than that of younger children. Indeed available data indicate high levels of protein-energy malnutrition and short-term hunger among school-age children.

Moreover, deficiencies of critical nutrients such as iodine, vitamin A and iron among the school-aged are pervasive. It is estimated that 60 million school-age children suffer from iodine deficiency disorders and that another 85 million are at risk for acute respiratory disease and other infections because they are deficient in vitamin A. The number suffering from iron deficiency anemia is greater still - 210 million. Parasitic worms that infect the intestines or the blood are a major source of disease and malnutrition in school-age children.

An estimated 320 million school-age children are infected with roundworm, 233 million with whipworm, and 239 million with hookworm. Schistosomiasis affects an estimated 200 million people throughout the world, approximately 88 million of whom are under 15 years old. Poor nutrition and health among schoolchildren contributes to the inefficiency of the educational system.

Children with diminished cognitive abilities and sensory impairments naturally perform less well and are more likely to repeat grades and to drop out of school than children who are not impaired; they also enroll in school at a later age, if at all, and finish fewer years of schooling. The irregular school attendance of malnourished and unhealthy children is one of the key factors in poor performance.

Even temporary hunger, common in children who are not fed before going to school, can have an adverse effect on learning. Children who are hungry have more difficulty concentrating and performing complex tasks, even if otherwise well nourished. Research and program experience shows that improving nutrition and health can lead to better performance, fewer repeated grades and reduced drop out.

School Feeding Programs are one of several interventions that can address some of the nutrition and health problems of school-age children. SFPs, and other school-based nutrition and health programs, can also motivate parents to enroll their children in school and to see that they attend regularly. Experience shows that properly designed and effectively implemented SFPs can:

— Alleviate short-term hunger in malnourished or otherwise well-nourished schoolchildren. This helps to increase the attention and concentration of students producing gains in cognitive function and learning.

— Motivate parents to enroll their children in school and have them attend regularly. When programs effectively reduce absenteeism and increase the duration of schooling, educational outcomes (performance, dropout, and repetition) improve.

— Address specific micronutrient deficiencies in school-age children. Most important of these are iodine and iron, which directly affect cognition. Meeting the iron and iodine needs of school-age children can translate into better school performance.

— Increase community involvement in schools, particularly where programs depend on the community to prepare and serve meals to children. Schools with their communities behind them are more effective than schools with less community involvement.

The number of hungry school-age children is unknown, but is likely to be a significant problem in various circumstances. Many factors contribute to hunger in schoolchildren : the long distances children have to travel to school, cultural meal practices that include no or small breakfasts or a lack of family time or resources to provide adequate meals to children before and/or during the school day. Simply alleviating this hunger in schoolchildren helps them to perform better in school.

In Jamaica providing breakfast to primary school students significantly increased attendance and arithmetic scores. The children who benefited most were those who were wasted, stunted, or previously malnourished. A US study showed the benefits of providing breakfast to disadvantaged primary school students. Before the start of a school breakfast program, eligible (low-income) children scored significantly lower on achievement testes than those not eligible. Once in the program, however, the test scores of the children participating in the program improved more than the scores of non-participants. The attendance of participating children also improved.

In Peru 23 malnourished and 29 well-nourished 9 to 11 year old boys were studied to assess the effects of breakfast on cognitive performance. Each boy served as his own control in a manner comparable to the Jamaica study cited above. Breakfast was a nutritionally fortified beverage and a baked grain product fortified with iron, similar to the meal provided in the government-sponsored school breakfast program.

A series of cognitive tests were administered in an experimental setting. Speed in performing a short-term memory test and discrimination of geometric patterns were improved under the breakfast condition in both groups. The effect was more pronounced in the nutritionally disadvantaged children.

Children in poor health start school later in life or not at all. A study in Nepal found that the probability of attending school was 5% for stunted children versus 27% for children of normal nutritional status. In Ghana malnourished children entered school at a later age and completed fewer years of school than better nourished children. The number of days that a child attends school is related to cognition and performance.

SFPs can have a positive effect on rates of enrollment and attendance. A recent evaluation of an on-going school feeding program in Burkina Faso found that school canteens were associated with increased school enrollment, regular attendance, consistently lower repeater rates, lower dropout rates in disadvantaged provinces, and higher success rates on national exams, especially among girls.

A small pilot school feeding program in Malawi was evaluated for its effect on enrollment and attendance. Over a three month period there was a 5% increase in enrollment and up to 36% improvement in attendance/absenteeism compared to control schools over the same period. Niger has one of the five lowest school enrollment rates in the world; the school feeding program is intended to enhance attendance of nomad and transhumant families, particularly of girls.

Beneficiaries receive the equivalent of the total daily recommended food intake in three meals per day. In addition, as an incentive for girls' participation in schools, some families receive an additional take-home ration. Evidence from past experience with the SFP shows that it contributes to its objectives: whenever canteens have been closed, even provisionally, immediate and high absenteeism follows and children are withdrawn from school. In areas with nomadic and transhumant populations, the school year cannot commence until food stocks arrive.

Although not a school feeding program in the traditional sense, school-based food distribution has also been used successfully to improve enrollment and attendance among school-age children, particularly girls. In Bangladesh a program of school-based food distribution increased enrollment by 20% versus a 2% decline in non-participating schools. In Pakistan, a programme provides an income transfer in the form of one or two tins of oil to families whose girls attend school for 20 days per month.

These food transfer mechanisms do not offer the same potential benefits, for example, meeting short-term hunger and specific nutritional needs, as programs that deliver food directly to beneficiaries. These kinds of programs should therefore be assessed within the context of other food and resource transfer programs.

Deficiencies of iron and iodine are among the most harmful types of malnutrition with regard to cognition. Iron deficiency renders children listless, inattentive and uninterested in learning. The research literature suggests a causal link between iron deficiency anemia and less than optimal behaviour for learning. Poor performance on a wide range of achievement tests among iron deficient children in school has been consistently documented.

In the case of iodine, most studies have focussed on the differences in cognitive test performance between children who lived in communities with and without endemic goiter. The results show differences in favor of the non-goiter areas. In Sicily, for example, the proportion of children with below-normal cognitive scores was 3% in areas with sufficient iodine, 18.5% in areas where iodine was inadequate, and 19.3% where iodine was inadequate and cretinism was endemic.

Studies in Indonesia and Spain have documented similar effects on children in areas with insufficient iodine. Fortification of school rations is the most efficient and effective route to alleviating micronutrient deficiencies in school children where SFPs are in operation. In South Africa, soup fortified with iron and vitamin C was provided to 350 schools in an area of low socio-economic development on the Cape Peninsula. Results showed that initially 12% of six to seven year old and 20% of 8 to 12 year old children had low weight-for-age, and 49% and 31% had low serum ferritin respectively.

At follow-up, after 15 weeks of intervention, iron status improved significantly; falling from 49% to 28% in 6 to 7 year old children and 31% to 21% in 8 to 12 year old children. A relatively new breakfast programme in Peru, which includes an iron-fortified ration, was evaluated for its short-term impact on diet, amongst other factors. The program significantly increased dietary intakes of energy by 25%, protein by 28% and iron by 46%.

A case-control study of the impact of providing heme-fortified cookies to school children in Chile found higher concentrations of hemoglobin among children receiving the fortified cookies through the school lunch programme. The impact was most significant among children with greater demands for iron such as post-menarchial girls and pubertal boys.

Schools that depend on the community to organize and implement SFPs offer certain advantages. These advantages include: increasing the contact, and hence communication, between parents and teachers, officials and others; giving parents the opportunity to become more aware of what goes on at schools; and serving to raise the value of education/the school for parents and the whole community. For example, school canteens are viewed as an important feature of education policy in Morocco.

Since 1978 WFP and the government have supported school feeding. The programs have strong government and community support and are viewed as part of a necessary package of inputs for improving education. The feeding program is credited with helping to maintain high enrollment and attendance and encouraging community participation in education. School cooperatives support the school canteens and parents associations assist with the transportation of food aid.

The research and program literature on SFPs shows the potential that school feeding has to contribute to improving education. These guidelines provide seven recommendations for improving the design and implementation of programs in order to meet some of this potential. The first recommendation, which calls for the establishment of a policy and objectives for school feeding programming, will provide the framework for implementing the subsequent recommendations.

These focus on the most critical aspects of school feeding programming including targeting, cost and financing issues, ration composition and meal delivery, program implementation, and monitoring and evaluation, and on the integration of feeding with other interventions that address the nutrition and health needs of schoolchildren.

School feeding programs are highly visible and as a result often have a significant political dimension, particularly since they can represent a considerable income transfer. This reality should not inhibit establishing a policy and objectives that will take advantage of the substantial potential for improving the impact of SFPs on education.

There is a built-in tendency toward universal coverage - providing meals for all schoolchildren -since all children in school throughout the day will require food. Furthermore, program coverage and targeting is always subject to a series of political, logistical, technical and informational constraints.

In view of the fact that resources are finite, particularly in the poorest countries, and that providing food is expensive, targeting is a critical element of any effort to improve the impact of a SFP on education. Targeting is essential if the program is to reach families and communities that lack the resources to adequately provide for their school-age children or those that need to be motivated to enroll their children in school and to have them attend more regularly.

The cost of school feeding programs is a major issue for both governments and donors. Feeding programs of any kind are expensive. Financing may include international assistance, but in all cases available public resources, or the potential to draw on them, are required. Cost alone can indicate little about the value of a SFP but, unfortunately, cost-effectiveness analyses, which assess costs relative to impact on nutrition and education outcomes are for the most part unavailable.

Nonetheless, implementing the recommendations in this guide should help to ensure that the benefit-side of the program is enhanced while controlling the cost side. Conditions in the education sector, such as levels of school enrollment, attendance, and performance, the availability of infrastructure and the capacity to implement different kinds of SFPs also need to be assessed. Information is also required on the community's perceptions and capacity to participate in school feeding programs.

Once school feeding programs are in place, altering them can meet strong resistance, however, a range of new experiences is now available that has the potential to alleviate some of the common obstacles to efficient and effective programming. Where a school feeding program already exists, a wealth of information is readily accessible; a critical step towards a better program is to thoroughly analyze this on-going experience.

Develop monitoring systems that focus on program processes, that is, how a program is functioning, and institute an evaluation system to assess the impact of the program on specific outcomes. Although many SFPs have been conceived out of ideological, political and economic pressures, the prejudices of international or national personnel, or even commercial or other non-objective influences, the first step toward an effective program is to build programs on sound and transparent objectives.

Since SFPs are highly visible and can offer a significant income transfer to families they will always be inherently political. To avoid the use of programs for political purposes, information on programs - especially, who the program is for and why and targeting measures-must be made readily available to the public.

Policy development and setting the objectives of school feeding provides the framework for implementing all the other recommendations aimed at improving the contribution that a SFP can make to education and better health and nutrition. The process of policy development calls for compiling information on: what 'food-related' and education-related problems exist in the school-age population which could be addressed by school feeding; where, geographically, the problems are located; and which school feeding options are available, or could be developed, for addressing these problems.

Analyzing the nutrition and health situation of school-age children has become a way to engage governments in the problems of this age group. The appropriate method of collecting information will vary by needs, circumstances and resources. Techniques include collecting routine statistics, making special surveys, conducting interviews, and holding focus group discussions with parents, teachers, students and health workers.

The idea is to generate a rapid assessment of the situation as opposed to implementing a protracted, expensive and bureaucratically complex study. The goal is to quickly grasp the problems and launch a discussion of the possible solutions within the context of the human and financial resources available in any given country.

World Food Programme has supported SFPs in the Gambia since 1971, providing a ration comprised of rice, wheat flour, canned meat, oil, and sugar. The programme has served on-site meals for about 92% of primary school children but resources for the programme have been diminishing as enrollments have increased. Program administrators have diluted rations in lieu of targeting to particular regions or schools, maintaining 92% coverage. An effort was made to produce local foods in school gardens as a way to increase supplies, however, these efforts have not been wholly successful.

The goal of targeting is to identify and reach families and communities that lack the resources to adequately provide for their school-age children. If the SFP is intended to motivate families to enroll children in school and to ensure more regular attendance, the target group is families whose children are not in school or who are frequently absent. Mechanisms and criteria for SFP targeting are similar in many cases to those used for other social programs: economic, geographic, and nutrition status.

In addition, specific education criteria such as overall enrollment, female enrollment, absenteeism, or student performance would also be included under some circumstances. In general it appears that SFP targeting is best done at the level of the school, or based on some other criteria - e.g., location - rather than on individual selection. The coverage of SFPs will depend on how many resources are available for programs and on the size of the problem that the program is intended to address.

Integrated Approaches to School Feeding Programmes

The new Indonesia SFP described above integrates deworming of students with feeding in participating schools. Earlier pilot efforts in Indonesia showed that combining deworming with the provision of food had an even greater impact on growth than when the food alone was provided.

In the state of Gujarat, India primary school students participating in a school meal program were provided with Albendazole along with the meal. The results of this program indicate a reduction in parasite infection from 71% to 40% with minimal additional costs since the SFP infrastructure was used for implementation. A new school feeding program in Bolivia is another example of the integrated approach to SFPs.

The program will include treatment of parasites, supplementation with micronutrients and Information, Education and Communication (IEC). Similarly, World Bank-assisted education projects in preparation in Haiti and Panama are integrating deworming and IEC in conjunction with improved targeting and delivery mechanisms for on-going SFPs.

The new SFP in Indonesia is providing between US $ 0.10 and US $ 0.15 per ration per day to village schools via the village bank. The guidelines for the relatively small, locally made ration are that it should contain 300 kcal and about 5 grams of protein. It will be provided three times a week for nine months. The key to the Indonesian programme is not only that it is a snack programme, intended to be additional to rather than replacing a family meal, but that the food is integrated with other interventions - deworming, health and nutrition education and water and sanitation.

In South Africa, a national school breakfast program takes a similar approach with decentralized management, provision of funds for local food purchases and integrated interventions. The estimated cost of the ration, which will provide about 25% of the recommended daily allowance

(RDA) for calories is about US $ 0.30 per child per day. An additional 10% per child per day is intended to cover local operating costs.

Bolivia's new USAID-assisted SFP is integrated with the educational reform underway in Bolivia. One objective of the reform is to increase parental involvement in education and the SFP is one mechanism for this. The municipalities will pay about US $ 1.60 per student per year and contribute to transportation costs of the donated foods from warehouses to schools. The total cost per child per year is estimated at US $ 4.00 for a snack programme consisting of fortified bread and hot chocolate. The programme will also integrate parasite treatment, health education and vision and hearing screening.

Economic or household income targeting is the most difficult of the targeting mechanisms available to implement, since measuring income is not straightforward, particularly where in-kind contributions to family income are substantial. Targeting is dependent on the availability of literate and numerate workers if bureaucratically administered income criteria are to be used.

Community leaders, teachers, local government entities or voluntary organizations can participate in identifying the poorest households, but this requires clear criteria that are transparent and not based on political favoritism. If economic targeting is already in place for other programmes, the school programme could build on it, however, singling out individual children in a classroom or school for a feeding programme or for a reduced price can be stigmatizing and socially and politically unacceptable.

Targeting by geographic area is most commonly used in school feeding programming. By using a poverty map, programming is restricted to certain administrative areas in which people have a high probability of being poor. This type of targeting does not require administrative intervention, but people who are outside of the area may move or travel distances to participate in the programme or may enroll their children in those schools. Changing established targeting criteria, usually restricting programmes to certain areas, can be difficult and may not be acceptable.

School feeding programming, particularly that supported by the WFP, has recently concentrated on addressing the need to encourage female enrollment and continuation in both primary and secondary school. Toward this end programmes are not only targeted at specific regions within countries where female participation in school is a problem, but the ration provided to girls may be of higher nutritional and caloric content to serve as an even greater incentive for girls to attend and stay in school.

In some cases the continuation of WFP-assisted programs is contingent on a certain proportion of girls participating in the program. SFPs, by virtue of the fact that they include food, are expensive. Beyond the costs of the food itself, the costs associated with food management, logistics and control can represent a significant financial burden for governments. On-site feeding is costly as it requires daily preparation and delivery of food, but is also a model that can invite, or require, community participation.

In response to the difficulties of on-site feeding and a new focus on delivering an appropriately-timed (with regard to effecting improvements in learning capacity) and high quality, consistent ration, some countries are developing programme models that include less costly commodities and more efficient systems for delivery to schools. Programmes that make good use of the education infrastructure for delivery and logistics will be most efficient.

The very fact that SFPs do not require, for the most part, additional infrastructure means that they can be less costly than other types of feeding programmes which distribute benefits to groups that are not in one location. Programmes that finance expensive kitchen equipment and supplies or build new infrastructure/canteens, however, will significantly raise the costs and lower the relative cost-effectiveness of programmes. Some SFPs are intentionally designed as an income-transfer for families, especially those that are trying to help attract girls to schools; the benefit received by families from these programmes must therefore surpass the costs of having their daughters away from home attending school.

A comparison of the costs of SFPs is problematic; the number of feeding days varies, as does the quantity of the rations and their quality. In the early 1990s two sizable studies made some accurate comparisons of cross-country cost information by standardizing and controlling for some of these differences.

Food aid is an important source of support for SFPs. There are high costs associated with transportation, warehouses and distribution; adequate storage facilities are required at every stage from port to the point of distribution. These costs are often borne by recipient governments. Management and distribution of food requires trained people to keep track of food inventories and their location, human resources may be as much of a constraint as cash and physical facilities. Nonetheless, if the economic and financial costs are acceptable then the cost of these programmes may not be prohibitive relative to the benefit provided.

Drawing on the private sector for school feeding programming overcomes many of the difficulties of on-site preparation of meals, and may be one of the least costly ways to feed children in schools. The private sector in this case can be street vendors, local canteen or a large canteen company (in cities and more commercially sophisticated areas). However, even these programmes incur costs in monitoring and supervision, and the start-up costs for developing school meal alternatives and making arrangements with vendors can be substantial.

Programs that utilize school canteens or street food vendors for school-based feeding programs may offer the most economical approach to school feeding. However, the technical and logistical implications, and hence costs in training and supplies to improve the provision of food through these sources are not insubstantial. Remarkably little concrete analysis has been done on this approach to school feeding.

Certain food selections are particularly expensive; foremost among these is milk, which is expensive per the number of calories, and nutrients it provides, and is perishable, which if figured in with the cost increases costs even further. UHT milk alternatives, which overcome the perishability issues, are particularly expensive to produce, especially in developing countries where the relevant technology is not widespread.

Parent-teacher or other community associations can play a significant role in a SFP and ultimately assume some of the costs. Efforts to strengthen parent-teacher organizations and increase the links between communities and schools are highly recommended, Targeting. Where feasible, more refined targeting mechanisms that maximize the participation of the most needy populations improve the efficiency of programmes. Ultimately this can mean charging fees to students who can afford them for participation in the programme.

Food transfer programmes cannot be considered 'sustainable' in the same way as, for example, a revolving credit programme, which ultimately pays for itself. A continual input of resources is required in order to provide food for school children. From the donor point of view, a programme may be seen as sustainable if the government commits to continuing the programme after donor support is removed. From the perspective of the individual beneficiary, the sustainable aspect of the programme is likely to be the lasting impact on behavior changes brought about through education or other interventions that are part of the program.

School meals provided early in the school day to alleviate hunger before or while classes are in session should help to improve attention, concentration, and achievement among children. Historically, and even now, political and social objectives dominate in school feeding programming. School meals were viewed, and in many cases still are, as a means for a school child to receive a large meal in the middle of the day, which typically coincides with local dietary practices.

These programmes served, and continue to serve, not only as nutrition programmes, but perhaps more as social welfare programs that provide a substantial economic benefit to the family since the child will not eat at mid-day from the family pot. Nonetheless, the nutritional quality and quantity of a ration should always be assessed as well as the effects of the timing of ration delivery. Other factors such as local food habits, logistical considerations, food availability, and cost will also influence the selection of the ration.

Rations that fill the actual micronutrient gaps in the diets of school-age children are higher in nutritional quality and can be expected to have greater impacts on learning. Ensuring that the appropriate level of micronutrients is included in the school ration may require more than selecting the appropriate mix of foods. Fortification may be an option if the size of the ration is relatively small, where the ration itself, or a component like flour, is centrally processed, or where the foods to be used do not contain a high level of the most critical micronutrients.

Fresh milk, although it appears to be nutritious and convenient, is not recommended as it is usually an expensive source of calories and is perishable and subject to contamination. A meal or snack provided early in the school day will eliminate hunger so that children are more attentive in class. In many cases the current emphasis on the timing of meals - providing the school meal early in the day to maximize the impact of the program on educational objectives- involves a significant change from current practice.

Furthermore, given the conditions for meal preparation in many developing countries - e.g., the need to utilize volunteers, long distances to fetch water and fuel for cooking, slow cooking facilities - the successful preparation and provision of meals to children early in the day is not easy. New program approaches have recently been developed and tested to overcome some of the technical and logistical obstacles associated with SFPs that countries might consider in developing new and modifying on-going programs:

Use of snack foods: Providing a snack as opposed to what may be a more traditional school meal (school lunch) will significantly cut the preparation time. In Indonesia, for example, a new programme will provide from 10 to 15 US cents per ration for the local production of a snack food with 300 kcal and 5 grams of protein. The intent of this programme is specifically to avoid industrially produced snack foods, since another objective is to increase local food production, however, the emphasis is equally on the delivery of an appropriately-timed snack.

The basic foods to be used are tubers (cassava sweet potato, taro), cereals (rice, corn), fruits, and vegetables. Snack foods also avoid the problem of substitution of the school meal for one of the family meals; this is preferable from a nutritional perspective since the school meal will be additional to the normal diet.

Products with quicker cooking times. Blended foods and cereal flours can be prepared much more quickly than unmilled whole grains. In Kenya, for example, a long-running programme that provided a school lunch to children involved more than 4 hours of preparation time. Unfortunately, although the foods were readily accepted and there were savings in fuel costs, this saving was canceled out by the 35% higher cost for transportation since the shelf life of products was much shorter.

Monetization is the sale of donated foods in the general market so that the central government can give the proceeds to school systems for feeding programmes; the school systems then purchase the food in their local communities. This practice obviates the need to transport large quantities of food around countries, which in many cases is a severe obstacle to implementing consistent and effective programmes. It also can increase the choice of food commodities that can be used in the feeding programme. This practice is becoming increasingly popular.

Although it generates income for the local economy, putting donated food in the market can depress indigenous food production and increase the risk of mismanagement and corruption. Issues of food preparation also need to be addressed.

The private sector. The off-site prepared meal/snack program addresses many of the technical and logistical concerns of SFPs. Programs in Peru and the Dominican Republic are examples of the private sector approach to school meals. In both cases the meal provided is a snack or breakfast which is itself a break from the traditional school lunch. Utilizing private enterprises to prepare and deliver the snack foods to schools facilitates the provision of the ration early in the day as well as ensuring a consistent and high quality ration while taking a minimal time away from learning. One problem with these programs can be the monotony of the ration.

The informal private sector/street vendors. Enlisting the support of local street vendors to provide better quality school meals to children is an option to consider. In Lesotho, for example, former local vendors who successfully bid to provide the privatized service run school canteens. In Nigeria, state and local governments train and license vendors who sell to schoolchildren. In other cases school principals exercise their authority locally and choose the vendors to serve their schools. A major concern that must be addressed in using this option is the quality and hygiene of the food served.

Information, education and communication (IEC) campaigns. Effective IEC programs which promote understanding of the benefits of providing meals earlier in the day and encourage the practices needed to realize early meal preparation, while addressing resistance to this approach, will help to encourage change to more cost-effective programs. Furthermore, it may be possible to alleviate hunger in schoolchildren without a formal feeding program. Encouraging and educating parents to feed their children before sending them to school or to provide a bag lunch or money for them to purchase food while at school may be an appropriate objective for IEC campaigns.

5

Challenges of Education

The Universal Declaration of Human Rights, adopted by the United Nations in 1948, asserted that 'everyone has a right to education', and subsequent international conferences and normative texts have reaffirmed this goal and sought to achieve it.

The World Conference on Education for All convened at Jomtien in 1990, addressed concerns about the inadequate provision of basic education, especially in the developing countries. The conference adopted the World Declaration on Education for All and agreed on a Framework for Action to Meet Basic Learning Needs.

The Declaration begins by affirming that 'every person – child, youth and adult – shall be able to benefit from educational opportunities designed to meet their basic learning needs' and then outlines an 'expanded vision' of basic education that can make this possible. The Framework for Action calls upon countries to adopt policies and practices that would ensure 'Universal access to, and completion of, primary education (or whatever higher level of education is considered as "basic") by the year 2000'. It also urges countries to pursue 'Improvement in learning achievement such that an agreed percentage of an appropriate age cohort (e.g., 80 per cent of 14-year-olds) attains or surpasses a defined level of necessary learning achievement'.

Achieving the goals embraced at Jomtien requires not only that children be admitted to school when they are of age, but that they complete the entire primary cycle and, equally important, actually learn at an appropriate level. It is generally agreed that at least four years of schooling are necessary for pupils to acquire the basic literacy and numeracy skills needed to become continuing learners, so the following analysis gives particular attention to the proportion of pupils completing Grade 4 or reaching Grade 5.

Considerable progress has been made over the last quarter century in expanding the capacity of primary school systems in all regions of the world. The overall number of primary school pupils rose from an estimated 396 million in 1970 to some 540 million in 1980 and to 650 million in 1995. If this rate of expansion were to continue, the number of pupils in the world's primary schools could reach 750 million by the year 2005 and 845 million by 2015.

Since the more developed countries and the countries in transition had already achieved universal primary education before 1970, the subsequent expansion in primary school enrolments is almost entirely attributable to gains in the developing countries, where the number of pupils increased from 305 million (representing 77 per cent of the global enrolment) in 1970 to 561 million (i.e., 86 per cent of the global enrolment) in 1995.

There is an upward trend in enrolments over the past twenty-five years in each of the less developed regions. This general trend is also evident in the improved net enrolment ratios between 1985 and 1995. These ratios take into account only those children who are in the official school age-group concerned, which varies from country to country. This expansion of enrolments generally outpaced population growth.

However, the total number of schoolage children not enrolled in school in the less developed regions rose from about 90 million in 1985 to some 110 million in 1990, before declining to about 83 million in 1995. Sub-Saharan Africa is the exception to this general trend: the number of unenrolled African children actually increased by 12 million between 1985 and 1995.

Unfortunately, growth in enrolments and school capacity has not been matched by gains in ensuring that pupils persist in their schooling and emerge from primary school with the knowledge and skills they need to function as workers, parents and citizens.

Today, in the less developed regions as a whole, only three out of four pupils can be expected to reach Grade 5, i.e. completing at least the four years of schooling generally considered necessary for achieving sustainable literacy skills. Thus the expected benefits of increased enrolments are being undermined by significant levels of drop-out, an acute symptom of school wastage.

No doubt the most serious and harmful wastage is evident in the 84 million primary-school-age children who are not enrolled in school, of which three out of five are girls. Another, but less evident, form of wastage concerns the pupils who complete the primary cycle but fail to gain the intellectual, social, cultural and ethical knowledge and skills that schooling should provide. Surveys in industrialized and developing countries alike have found, for example, that substantial proportion of children complete their primary-school education without acquiring even an adequate mastery of reading. Children who never gain access to school and those who enrol but do not attain an adequate level of learning constitute tragic waste of the human, social and economic potential of the countries concerned.

A more narrow, operational definition of school wastage refers to pupils who do not complete their schooling in the prescribed number of years either because they drop out of school entirely or because they repeat one or more grades.

Of course, wastage is also a serious problem in non-formal education programmes, such as adult literacy courses. However, data on such programmes are not readily available and the issues involved are often quite different from those affecting schooling.

A major objective of Education for All is to ensure that children throughout the world have access to basic education, actually acquire basic literacy and numeracy skills, and develop the capacity for autonomous learning. Since the resources made available to schools for this important mission are often inadequate, they need to be efficient in moving pupils through each cycle of education in a timely fashion. For the purpose of measuring the 'internal efficiency' of a school system, it is generally assumed that all pupils entering Grade 1 should complete the primary school cycle within a prescribed number of years. To the extent that pupils drop out of school or repeat grades, the system is considered inefficient.

Primary School Enrolments: Current Trends

While great progress has been made in the 1990s in getting around 10 million more children into school each year, a formidable challenge remains to be met. However, we need to see this achievement in the context of slower expansion in the 1980s that leaves sub-Saharan Africa with a lower proportion of its children in school in 1997 than in 1980.

There are many problems in measuring efforts towards universal primary education. These include the different enrolment figures, accuracy and the internal efficiency of the school system in retaining children and allowing them to progress smoothly through the curriculum. It should also be noted that formal primary schooling is just one facet of 'Education for All'; efforts at adult education and informal education are important for those unable to benefit from the school system.

The large number of children still out of school live mainly in sub-Saharan Africa and south Asia. However, there are many problems in estimating this number. The most worrying fact is that there are indications that sub-Saharan Africa will soon contain the largest proportion of children out of school despite having a population of only half the size of south Asia.

There is great variety across regions in their progress towards universal primary education. Sub-Saharan Africa, south Asia and the Arab states have the weakest enrolment figures. Within regions, differences in enrolments must be seen in the light of diverse facts about a country.

The general level of poverty is an important correlate, as is the level of urbanization amongst the population. Girls' education suffers the effect of household and state poverty more than boys, especially in south Asia. The number of female teachers, especially at secondary level, also has an important effect on girls' education.

The quality of education affects the level of achievement of pupils. Quality education requires decent expenditure, adequate numbers of well-trained teachers, and reasonably resourced schools. Quality education is necessary to increase enrolment where children face many obstacles in coming to school.

Since the 1960s it has been the goal of governments and international agencies to ensure that all children in the world receive a basic education. In 1990 this challenge was formalized at the World Conference on Education for All in Jomtien, Thailand, where delegates pledged to reach the goal of universal access to primary education by the year 2000. While that challenge still remains, the recent follow-up conference in Dakar noted that there had been some significant improvements: "On a worldwide scale, the total number of primary school pupils rose from just under 600 million to over 680 million over the decade, and the percentage of children in school edged upwards, from 80 per cent to 84 per cent."

The progress noted at Dakar must be seen against the background of the 1980s, when educational spending was reduced (often by freezing teacher's salaries) and expansion was thwarted. The number of children in school was increased by almost 10 million a year in the 1990s, which is almost twice the annual increase recorded in the 1980s of about 5.7 million children.

This poor trend was caused by worldwide recession, which impoverished both states and private households, and the implementation of structural adjustment programmes that constrained expenditure on public services.The effect was particularly strong in sub-Saharan Africa where educational spending dropped dramatically, and the enrolment ratios for many countries in the late 1980s were below what they had been in 1980.

Even in 1997, sub-Saharan Africa had not managed to catch up with its position in 1980. Although a great many more children have been enrolled, the population increase means that the percentage of children in school compared to the total number of children is less than 17 years before.

Table 1 we sum up global trends over the last two decades, showing that while the absolute numbers of children in school have grown in that period, large numbers of children are still not getting to school. The largest numbers, revealed by the relatively poor enrolment rates, are in South Asia and sub-Saharan Africa, but rates also remain low in the Arab world.

Table 1: Primary school enrolments (millions) and gross enrolment ratios

	1980		1990		1997	
	Numbers	GER	Numbers	GER	Numbers	GER
World	541.6	95.9	596.9	99.2	668.5	101.8
Europe	52.5	102.2	49.0	101.1	46.3	104.7
East Asia and Oceania	210.9	110.4	194.9	118.5	214.7	118.0
Latin America&Caribbean	65.4	104.1	75.5	105.0	85.2	113.6
Arab States	20.8	79.0	30.4	81.4	36.6	84.7
South Asia	96.1	75.9	136.0	90.3	157.7	95.4
Sub-Saharan Africa	50.5	79.5	64.4	74.8	81.0	76.8

These global figures only tell us part of the story. To fill out the picture we need to see what the gross enrolment ratio reveals and conceals and to look for a measure of how well schools perform, once children are enrolled.

The Gross Enrolment Ratio (GER) is the total number of pupils enrolled in a level of education regardless of age, expressed as a percentage of the corresponding eligible agegroup in the population. But a GER of above 100 does not mean that every child is being properly educated. A high GER could mean that many children are repeating the same class over again or are entering school at the wrong age and for the wrong length of time.

As countries move towards universal education their GER is likely to be above 100%; children above the formal age for primary education are often still in primary school, swelling the numbers and pushing up the ratio. However, the GER is the best measure of the capacity of a country's school system as it measures the total amount of children in school compared with the total amount who should be in school.

The Net Enrolment Ratio (NER) is a more accurate measure of how close a country is to Universal Primary Education as it only counts children of the correct age. However, more often than not we do not know the net enrolment ratio. It is possible to calculate a net enrolment ratio only where we have good census data, showing the size of each age cohort, and as good information about the ages of children in school.

Good figures are often not available, so that gross enrolment ratios remain the available figures, used by ministries of education, and the only realistic way of making international comparisons. Even where 100% of the age group enroll in primary school, a country may not be achieving universal primary education. This is because many children drop-out before completing the full cycle of primary education.

There are also a large number of children who are made to repeat years, making them less likely to complete the full primary curriculum. The number of drop-outs and repeaters effect the 'internal efficiency' of the school system. So, while children in Europe are almost certainly destined to complete five years of primary education at least, half the children in India who enroll in the first class will drop-out before reaching grade five. In Madagascar this percentage is even higher and 34% of those in primary school are actually repeating a grade rather than usefully progressing through the school system.

Table 2: Internal Efficiency of school system in selected countries in 1996.

Selected country	*Survival rate to grade 5*	*Children repeating a grade*
India	52%	4%
Indonesia	88%	6%
Venezuela	89%	10%
Madagascar	40%	34%
Ethiopia	51%	8%
Morocco	75%	12%
Italy	99%	0%
Finland	100%	0%

Over the last decade or so the emphasis on formal schooling as a compulsory right for all children has developed and changed. Lifelong learning with an emphasis on skills for life and for development is now the primary aim. The Dakar declaration included a target for adult education as well as for children.

Formal schooling is just one facet of the challenge of education for all, which involves reaching those outside the school system. We should not ignore the achievements of non-formal education (night schools and drop-in schools) for those unable to commit to regular primary schooling. Many non-government organizations work for education as well as other economic and social goals with the poorest children and adults.

One of the most well known projects of this type is BRAC (Bangladesh Rural Advancement Committee) which reached 1.1 million children by 1996, in 35, 000 schools for 8-10 year olds. It specifically targets children of poor families who have never been to school or have dropped out of school.

Similarly, in Latin America, the Escuela Nueva project in Colombia, (as well as the attempts to replicate it in other countries of the region), have shown that NGO approaches can expand opportunities for basic education. But these are very much exceptions and have seldom been successfully transplanted across frontiers; there is nothing on the scale BRAC, for example, elsewhere in south Asia. The main burden of responsibility for reaching the targets for education for all rests with governments.

The pressure of population increase Although the numbers of children in school are increasing rapidly, by around 80 million in the last decade, demographic trends experienced by many developing countries means that absolute numbers out of school are harder to change.

Changes in enrolment ratios for different countries and regions are vitally dependent on the increase in the number of school age children. The two areas with the highest fertility rates, South Asia (3.5 births per woman) and sub-Saharan Africa (5.6 births per woman) have had the greatest difficulty in achieving Universal Primary Education.

It was agreed at Dakar in April 2000 that there are still 113 million children out of school in 1998.However, this is a rather different number to many earlier estimates, which reveals the difficulties in gathering accurate statistics. While there is currently international agreement on this figure, it is by no means 'right'.

The UNESCO Institute of Statistics had estimated in 1995 and 1998 that the number of out-of-school children in 1995 was the rather larger figure of 145 million in the age group 6-11. Elsewhere, a UNESCO report from 1999 quotes the figure as 83 million in 1995.

The World Bank has a much smaller figure of 68 million children out-of-primary-school in 1997 in its World Education Indicators, although strangely these are based apparently on UNESCO figures. Recently, however, the institution has agreed to the Dakar figures. OXFAM, on the other hand, is currently using a 125 million figure in its campaigning material.

The different estimates come from the different methods of calculation, whether using official UN statistics, or those gathered for the conference, or using data only in the 6-11 age-group rather than the whole primary age group in various countries.

The wide disparity in the estimates highlights the enormous problems associated with the formation of these statistics, which rely on an accurate knowledge of the school age population. They also give an air of unreality to plans that are based upon them. From all the attempts at estimation, however, two conclusions can be drawn which would seem to hold true whether we take the higher or lower figures:

The largest number of out of school children in the 1990s were living in South Asia. Because of an enormous population and weak enrolment ratios, this region has always contained the largest total number of children out of school. Between 31 million in 1997 according to World Bank education indicators, and 46 million in 1998 according to the calculations made in Dakar, these are both higher numbers than calculations for any other region.

A growing proportion of the world's out of school children are in sub-Saharan Africa. This is a worrying trend as Africa has a much smaller population. It is the only region in the world that has actually seen an increase in the number of children out of school. The latest estimate from Dakar, sees sub-Saharan Africa on the verge of overtaking South Asia with 42 million children out of school in 1998. Thus, while the largest number of children out of school is in south Asia, sub-Saharan Africa now has the highest proportion of children deprived of primary education.

How close are regions to achieving universal primary education? When we look at how close regions are to achieving universal primary education we see that:

Sub-Saharan Africa has the poorest enrolment ratios and is furthest away from achieving Universal primary education. The overall sub-Saharan African Gross Enrolment ratio has only gained two percentage points since 1990. As has already been noted, this is actually a lower percentage of children in school than in 1980. In 1997, the Net Enrolment ratio was 56 percent. This means that roughly only half of African primary school children are enrolled in primary school at the right age and progress smoothly through the grades.

South Asia has poor enrolment figures but has experienced improvement. While enrolment figures in South Asia look better, they still represent an enormous number of children out of school. South Asia has achieved a 5 percent increase in Gross Enrolment ratio in the 1990s. The Net Enrolment ratio in 1997 is still very low, however, at 78 percent.

The Arab states have low enrolment figures and do not show much improvement. The Arab states do particularly badly in getting their children enrolled, as they have gross enrolment ratios lower than South Asia. However, they represent an economically more developed region, with an average Gross National Product per capita of $1,754 compared to $452 for South Asia and $522 for sub-Saharan Africa. This may because of a highly unequal distribution of wealth or because of a low value placed in formal education in Islamic cultures. The Net Enrolment ratio in 1997 is actually a percentage point higher, indicating that children do not tend to repeat a grade or enter school at the wrong age in this region.

Table 3: Net and Gross Enrolment ratios in 1990 and 1997

	NER 1990	GER 1990	NER 1997	GER 1997
World	80	99	88	102
Europe	-	104	-	107
East Asia and Oceania	-	119	-	118
Latin America & Caribbean	-	105	93	114
Arab States	-	81	86	85
South Asia	-	90	78	95
Sub-Saharan Africa	-	75	56	77

GER figures from UNESCO World Education Report, NER figures from UNDP Human Development Report 2000.

However, there is great variation within these regions. For instance, despite the considerable achievements in south Asia within the last decade, there remains stark differences between countries of the region and within them. In Bhutan in 1998, for example, half the children were out of school, while within India net enrolments of over 90 per cent in Assam contrasted with less than 50 per cent in Uttar Pradesh.

In sub-Saharan Africa more than 10 countries have Gross Enrolment ratios of more than 90%, including Lesotho, Madagascar, Malawi, Mauritius, Namibia, Nigeria, Botswana, Republic of the Congo, Gabon, South Africa, Togo and Zimbabwe. However, many of these education systems are undermined by very high drop out and repetition rates and only South Africa, Mauritius and Malawi are very close to achieving Universal Primary Education.

But education systems are indicative of other factors that keep children from school and states from increasing their expenditure on education. If we look at the ten countries with the worst Gross Enrolment ratios we can see that they fare very badly in other indicators of wealth and human development.

The level of urbanization of a country is also an important factor, partly as a correlate of Gross National Product but also because rural areas within countries tend to be poorer, there are fewer economic opportunities for educated people to act as an incentive for schooling, and there is a bigger demand for child labour in agriculture.

While poverty, both of the household and of the state, has the largest effect on levels of schooling, it has a differential impact on boys and girls. Girls' schooling seems to suffer additionally, and in nearly every country or region the level of girls' enrolment and retention is lower. Looking at the percentage of female enrolments in primary and secondary education across regions allows us to draw certain conclusions:

Overall the low enrolment of girls at primary school has not improved in the 1990s. The percentage of female enrolment at primary school has remained the same at 46% and has only shown a percentage increase at the secondary level. Latin America and the Caribbean actually have better female enrolment at the secondary level. This region is unusual in that it appears that girls are doing better in the education system than boys, a phenomenon that is now also being reported within Europe.

Gender equity in the Arab states is weak and has not much improved. While 45% of secondary school enrolments are female as compared to 42% in 1990, at the primary school level, gender equity has only slightly increased with 45 % of enrolments being girls. If we combine this with the low enrolment ratio for this region, we see that a large number of girls are out of school. Gender Equity in sub-Saharan Africa is also bad. Sub-Saharan Africa shows a low figure, similar to the Arab states, with worse gender equity at the secondary level and little improvement over the decade.

South Asia has the worst record for gender equity Only 42% of children at primary school are girls and only 38 % of secondary school children enrolled are girls. Nor do these enrolment figures take account of the numbers of drop-outs which are also higher amongst girls.

In many cultures, the supply of women teachers is critical to the expansion of education for girls. This is especially so at the secondary level. They are needed not only to teach girls, especially where single-sex schools are the norm, but also as role models to girls and as support within schools. While women worldwide are prevalent in the teaching profession, (58% primary and 48% secondary), in the areas where the gender divide is large, the number of teachers at secondary level is often only a small percentage.

Table 4: Percentage of enrolments who are girls at Primary and Secondary levels.

	1990		1997	
	Primary Enrolments (percentage female)	Secondary Enrolments (percentage female)	Primary Enrolments (percentage female)	Secondary Enrolments (percentage female)
World	46	44	46	45
Europe	49	49	49	49
East Asia and Oceania	47	43	48	46
Latin America&Caribbean	49	51	48	52
Arab States	44	42	45	45
South Asia	41	36	42	38
Sub-Saharan Africa	45	43	45	44

In South Asia there is a low percentage of women teachers at both primary and secondary level. Often in rural areas there are even fewer women teachers. Both these factors are a constraint on attempts to achieve gender equity.

Table 5: Percentage of teaching staff female at primary and secondary levels

	Primary level	Secondary level
World	58%	48%
Sub-Saharan Africa	43%	31%
Arab States	52%	42%
Southern Asia	32%	37%

As countries raise the level of enrolment, it is important that this is not at the expense of an acceptable level of quality. While there is not enough research into what factors affect quality, and it is apparently hard to establish a reliable correlation between many factors and school achievement, the following are probably important:

Expenditure: Across the world there is great variance in the amount spent on education per pupil. The expenditure per student as a percentage of the Gross National Product shows what a government's commitment to education is. But even where a poor country shows a reasonably large commitment to education the total amount will be small if the Gross National Product for that country is low. As more than 90% of the education budget goes on teacher salaries, however, the dynamics of each education system, which have different levels of teacher pay, need to be examined in depth.

Pupil/teacher ratio: Out of 23 countries listed as having a pupil/teacher ratio of above forty in 1997, 19 were in sub-Saharan Africa.However, there is little research evidence that can conclusively prove that lowering the ratio of teachers to pupils will be a cost-effective measure to increase quality.It may be that large class sizes are a good way for the education system to expand initially, however, the highest quality education will only be achieved with smaller class sizes.

Teacher Training: Teachers need to have the requisite academic qualifications and some teacher training in order to have a high quality education system. Only 73 % of teachers in Sub-Saharan Africa, and only 70% of teachers in South and West Asia have teaching qualifications that certify them to teach according to national standards.

Resources: Many primary schools in poorer countries remain pitifully underresourced. In studies of factors that affect school achievement, this is often found to be the most important influence on quality.In a pilot UNESCO-UNICEF survey of least developed countries in 1995 it was found that, in most countries, one third or more of students gathered in classes without even a useable chalkboard. In more than half the countries, over 90 % of the pupils in the final grade of primary education did not have a textbook in their mother tongue.

The 'quantity' of education affects the availability of education, and particularly the problem of providing schooling in rural areas, where children often do not go to school because of the distance they must walk to school. However, possibly the largest number of out-of school children do not go to school because they are unable or unwilling to make the economic effort. It may not be culturally or socially acceptable for girls to go to school, especially if they have had an early marriage or are past puberty.

However, it is more likely that families cannot afford the costs of fees, books or clothing, or they cannot afford the lost labour time and the opportunity for wages. Often children drop out because of a perceived lack of economic benefit in basic education and a low level of expectation of achievement at a higher level. Low levels of economic development are integrally linked to low demand for schooling. It may be a greater challenge to encourage families to send their children to school than to provide universal access to primary schooling.

Little is really known about how to raise the demand for schooling. It is probable that increasing the opportunities for educated people, or the material condition of families would have the largest affect on demand for schooling. Parents usually do not cite low quality schooling as a factor in their decision not to send their children to school.

However, this may be attributed to them not having a better school to compare it to, much education themselves, or having little contact with the school. We can speculate that higher quality schooling may encourage children to come to school in a number of ways:

— *Children are likely to be more attracted to a school with better facilities.* Where children have to renegotiate labour and household chores, or must work to help pay for their education, then schooling that is enjoyable is likely to make a difference. Children who receive more individual attention may be better motivated.

— *Children are less likely to drop out if they are receiving a high enough quality education to pass through the grades rather than repeat years.* Large numbers of repeaters are usually accompanied by high levels of drop-out. Children loose motivation if they do not feel they are progressing.

— *Children are likely to continue with their education if they achieve well.* Gaining the necessary standard to move on to secondary school raises the likelihood of economic empowerment through education.

— *Higher levels of achievement may increase expectations for younger siblings and children.* Greater educational achievement may have a long-term affect on the levels of literacy of younger members of the family and their desire and expectation for education.

Dropping-out

An obvious and blatant form of wastage involves pupils who start school but drop out before they reach a level of sustainable literacy and numeracy. Drop-out at the primary level is virtually non-existent in industrialized countries because they enforce compulsory education laws.

In the less developed regions, however, early drop-out is a major problem. Of the approximately 96 million pupils who entered school for the first time in 1995, one quarter (24 million) are likely to abandon their schooling before they reach Grade 5.

Avialable statistics shows that boys persist in school at slightly higher rates than do girls, except in Latin America and the Caribbean, and in the more developed regions. However, the more important disparity between boys and girls is evident in the overall enrolment figures for the less developed regions.

Three-quarters of the 8 million school entrance-age children who did not enter school in 1994-95 were girls. This gender disparity at the beginning of schooling generally continues throughout the primary cycle, as can be seen in the gap between the net enrolment ratios of boys and girls.

Much dropping out of school occurs between the first and second grades. In the less developed regions taken together, nearly half of all drop-out occurs before pupils reach Grade 2. The exception is the Arab States, where the overall survival rate to Grade 5 is high, but most drop-out occurs between Grades 4 and 5.

The pattern of substantial drop-out occurring at the beginning of the primary school cycle is particularly distressing because pupils with only a year or two of schooling leave in a state near illiteracy. However, the overall survival rates to Grade 5 appear to be improving in a number of countries for which data are available.

Repeating Grades

Another form of school wastage occurs when pupils have to repeat grades. In developing countries especially, this is often a prelude to drop-out. School systems around the world differ widely in their policies toward pupils who fail to master the work appropriate to a particular grade level. In a majority of countries, both developed and developing, educators require such pupils to repeat the grade in order to give them additional time to learn material that they failed to master the first time around. Repetition is thus seen as a remedy for slow learners.

The practice is typically applied in Grade 1 out of a conviction that it is important for pupils to get off to a good start in their education. However, repeating the final primary grade is also widespread in countries where admission to secondary school is based on passing an end-of-primaryschool examination.

A minority of countries appear to believe that repetition creates more problems than it solves and therefore follow a policy of automatic promotion. Accordingly, pupils proceed to the next grade even when they have not mastered the material of the previous grade. Some educators argue that pupils who did not learn something the first time are not likely to benefit from repeating the same academic year. A wiser policy, they argue, is to provide such pupils additional assistance and allow them to proceed to the next grade with their peers.

In the less developed regions together, about eight per cent of all pupils enrolled in primary school around 1995 were repeaters, and nearly one out of three pupils in Grade 1 was a repeater. Overall repetition rates are highest in sub-Saharan Africa and in Latin American and the Caribbean.

Because the incidence of repetition is largely determined by the attitudes and practices of educators in each country, the magnitude of repetition can vary considerably even among countries of comparable levels of educational and economic development. For example, Niger and Madagascar are both in the sub-group of least developed countries: each has a large proportion of people living on less than US$1 a day and a primary net enrolment ratio of less than 50 per cent. Nevertheless, Niger has a repetition rate of only 16 per cent, compared with 32 per cent in Madagascar.

Repetition rates appear to be declining in many developing countries. The percentage of pupils repeating their present grade declined between 1985 and 1995 in all less developed regions. However, this general trend did not apply to the sub-set of least developed countries, where the percentage of repeaters increased.

Repetition, like drop-out, tends to be more prevalent in the first and in the final grades of the primary school cycle, but repetition patterns vary considerably both within and between different countries) and across the several regions. In general, however, the percentage of repeaters in Grade 1 exceeds the percentage of repeaters in all grades together. The proportion of pupils reaching Grade 5 without repeating a grade also varies widely among countries.

Under optimal circumstances, every primary-school pupil would spend one year at each grade level and complete a five-year cycle in five years, or a sixyear cycle in six years, and so on. When pupils repeat grades or drop out, however, the average number of 'pupil-years' required to move pupils through the cycle exceeds the prescribed number of years.

In many countries the proportion of wastage due to drop-out as compared to repetition differs for boys and girls. For example, drop-out is a more significant factor for girls than for boys in countries such as Indonesia, Senegal, Guinea and Togo, whereas it is more important factor for boys than for girls in Colombia and Lesotho.

Cost of School Wastage

Wastage substantially reduces the capacity of school systems to meet the objectives of education for all. Pupils who require more than one year to complete a grade take up space, teaching time, textbooks and other resources that could be devoted instead to other pupils. In Cambodia, for example, where four out of every ten pupils at any given time are repeaters, the Asian Development Bank estimated that serving these repeaters requires 10,000 additional teachers and 5,000 more classrooms, i.e. 20 per cent of the existing stock. Furthermore when many pupils repeat grades, some classes become abnormally large, making the teaching and learning conditions difficult for everyone. Wastage has important long-term effects on patterns of adult illiteracy.

It is widely recognized that children who drop out of school before acquiring basic literacy and numeracy skills frequently relapse into illiteracy. Estimates based on a simulation model project that 57 per cent of the illiterate adults (aged 15 and over) constituting the target population for literacy instruction in the less developed regions over the period 1995-2005 would comprise the backlog of adults who were illiterate at the beginning of the period. Another 21 per cent would be children reaching age 15 during the period and who had no access to schooling, while 22 per cent more would be children reaching age 15 and dropping out of school before reaching Grade 5.

One of the presumed benefits of repetition is to ensure that pupils in each grade have attained more or less the same level of learning and can learn at about the same pace. This assumption is frequently undermined, however, when teachers end up dealing with pupils of varying ages.

A recent report on the age of pupils by grade in Latin America shows that Grade 1 teachers had pupils ranging in age from 5 to 8, while a similar study in Kenya revealed an age range in Grade 1 from 2 to 16. In some countries, the age range found in the early grades is due both to repetition and to the practice of admitting children who are younger and older than the official entry age.

Many teachers and school administrators consider it normal for substantial proportions of pupils to be held back. They take pride in high repetition rates and see them as evidence of their commitment to high standards. Other educators, however, see them as an indictment of the teaching that the retained pupils received. In any case, what some see as a yardstick of academic quality can have pedagogical, social and personal consequences that are quite destructive.

Anecdotal evidence suggests that decisions to hold pupils back are sometimes made on capricious and arbitrary grounds that have little to do with actual pupil performance. Teachers often favour pupils who readily follow rules and give more attention to the brightest pupils at the expense of the others, including pupils who are competent but not outstanding.

A study carried out in rural primary schools in Honduras, for example, found that 20 per cent of pupils with sufficient qualifications had not been promoted, while another study in rural Brazil found no significant relation between actual performance and promotion. School systems in many countries lack clear definitions and established procedures for assessing pupil performance and making promotion decisions.

By operating in an elitist fashion and failing to be sensitive to the needs of many ordinary and low-achieving pupils, schools cease to be truly open and accessible to ali. They become the property of a minority of highly motivated local elites and thus become alienated from the community as a whole. Schools that limit the prospects for success undermine the motivation of parents to send their children to school.

Maintaining policies that lead to repetition of grades by large numbers of pupils is expensive. The cost of repetition alone was estimated to total at least US$6 billion for all regions together, with Latin America and the Caribbean region accounting for about half of the total. The cost of total wastage in the first four grades was estimated to absorb some 16 per cent of public current expenditure on education in the less developed regions. These estimates should be viewed as minimal because they do not take into account capital expenditure on education, nor private spending.

Regardless of its pedagogical effects, repeating grades is inefficient because it increases the per pupil cost of schooling without increasing the number of graduates produced. Resources devoted to a repeater are resources that could have been used either to permit another child to enter school or to improve the quality of instruction for pupils already there.

One of the premises of investment in education is that it makes an important and measurable contribution to the economic growth of society, in particular by improving the productivity of labor. A close parallel exists between the rate of economic growth of a country and the overall level of education of its active population. This correlation has been documented both in advanced industrial societies and in developing countries where the agricultural sector remains dominant.

Whereas reliance on agriculture has frequently been a force for keeping children out of school, modern agricultural practices require more skilled, albeit fewer, workers. In view of the importance of the agricultural sector for the economy of most poor countries, it is clear that the persistence of substantial school wastage is contrary to the economic interest of these countries, especially since wastage tends to be more pronounced in rural than in urban areas. Although the level of education is not the only factor involved in agricultural production, the failure to enable many rural young people to master basic skills undermines other initiatives to stimulate rural development.

Children who drop out of school before acquiring sustainable reading and writing skills frequently relapse into illiteracy. Thus dropping out undermines efforts to reduce adult illiteracy – like trying to drain a sink that is being filled at the same time by the tap. Children and adolescents out of school in urban areas are also more vulnerable to the attractions of street life and organized gangs of children, which contributes to problems of delinquency and crime. Furthermore, school wastage promotes a 'culture of failure'. Pupils who are unable to proceed with their classmates to the next grade frequently face problems of self-esteem and are likely to develop negative attitudes toward schooling. Repeaters thus become likely candidates for dropping out entirely.

Children's success in school is generally believed to be primarily a function of their innate intellectual aptitudes. Yet, in the case of pupils who come from deprived home environments, their living conditions may considerably reduce their motivation and opportunities to learn, whatever their intellectual ability may be. Also, the language of instruction may put certain children at a distinct disadvantage. By disregarding these conditions and attributing poor academic performance to the assumed 'inability' of the child, the school merely reinforces discriminatory social conditions.

Data from UNESCO and other sources show that drop-out rates are highly sensitive to the national economic context. Studies in certain less developed countries, for example, have shown a significant and positive correlation between drop-out rates and the percentage of people living below the poverty line, i.e. on less than $1 a day.

Shool wastage correlates also with several educational, social and demographic variables. For instance, as access to health services increases, so does the survival rate to Grade 5. As one would expect, children do better in school when they are healthy.

Countries with similar social indices sometimes report quite different patterns of repetition, while countries at quite different levels of development tend to have dissimilar levels of dropout. It appears that drop-out rates are closely linked to the general state of a society – its level of economic and cultural development, how social services are distributed and attitudes toward education –

while the repetition rates are largely determined by school policies.

Even when public schools are ostensibly free, parents must bear various direct costs to educate their children. Often, they must purchase school supplies and textbooks. While school uniforms may be a source of pride for pupils and their families, they can represent a major cost for parents with limited means.

Developing countries frequently impose de facto tuition charges in the form of fees for registration, examinations and other services. In many cases these 'user fees' total many times the amount the government's expenditure per pupil. Public policy-makers can reduce these direct costs that families must bear to enrol their children in school through means such as subsidizing textbooks and transportation, providing essential school supplies and waiving school fees for pupils from very poor families. Recently, for example, in response to the economic crisis, Indonesia obtained a rescue programme from the World Bank and the Asian Development Bank to help keep some 25 million Indonesian pupils in school over the next five years.

Families also face indirect costs, primarily in the form of labour that the child would otherwise be performing if not enrolled in school. Thus, pupils in school cannot be taking care of younger siblings in the home or selling goods in the market or looking after farm animals or working in the fields.

A study of school wastage conducted in twenty-four schools in the eleven counties of the State of Bahia in Brazil showed that the primary cause of school-drop-out was the need for the child to work to help support the family. A report prepared for the Egyptian Ministry of Education in

1993 estimated that more than 1.5 million children under the age of 15 formed part of the working population.

Both the direct and indirect costs of schooling are particularly important in the case of girls. When poor families conclude that they can afford to educate only some of their children, they tend to favour sons over daughters in the belief that it is more important for boys to be equipped to enter the job market. In some countries, it is common for the eldest daughter to drop out of school as soon as there are younger brothers and sisters for her to look after and she is unlikely to return to school even if the younger siblings, both male and female, enter school.

Lack of proximity to schools is an important cause of wastage, especially for younger children in rural areas who need a school close to their homes. Some countries are overcoming this obstacle by setting up community schools or 'branch' or 'feeder' schools connected to established schools. Even though these small schools often can offer only the first few primary grades, they can have a positive impact on access, especially for girls.

A UNESCO survey in 1991 showed that the proportion of incomplete schools in rural areas was over 30 per cent in nearly half of the countries of sub-Saharan Africa and in one-third of the Arab States and countries in the Latin America and Caribbean region. However, the pupils who enter these incomplete schools often find it difficult to continue their schooling at a more distant location. If there is no provision of school transport or midday meals, only the most motivated families will continue sending their children to school away from the local community. A few countries, such as Bhutan, Malaysia and Thailand, are overcoming this difficulty by providing limited boarding facilities for pupils who live great distances from school, but this solution is more often used for postprimary levels of education.

Another approach to expanding access, used in the Philippines and Thailand, for example, is to employ 'mobile teachers' who travel by horseback or other means to reach pupils in remote areas. Yet another approach that is used in thinly populated areas is to permit teachers to teach several grades simultaneously – multigrade instruction.

To be effective, this approach requires ample availability of teaching materials, since pupils must spend a good part of the school day working on their own or in small groups while the teacher is working with pupils in other 'grades'. The provision of adequate classrooms and teachers in accessible schools is an important condition for universal primary education, but other, complementary measures have proved necessary to ensure that all children actually attend school. Parents need to be encouraged and convinced to send their children to school and compulsory education laws need to be enforced. Child labour laws that are in conformity with international standards and that are rigorously enforced tend to ensure that children are not kept out of school.

Changing Educational Policies

Children are far more likely to be motivated to learn and to persist in school if the curricula and teaching methods are of high quality. By contrast, pupils who are bored and fail to see the connection between their personal lives and what they are taught in school become candidates for academic failure and, eventually, dropping out. There is much that can and must be done to improve the quality of instruction through a concerted strategy to improve the curricula, the training of teachers and the reorganization of the school to promote learning. The involvement and leadership of the school head can make or break any attempt at reform, as the experience of Chile's 900 Schools Programme shows. There, school directors and programme supervisors devise an annual improvement plan to examine their needs, raise their standards and, in co-operation with teachers, evaluate their work.

Numerous studies have established that skilled teaching has a strong positive impact on pupil achievement. For example, a recent study in rural Pakistan found that investments that improve teacher quality and increase student exposure to teachers are likely to have higher returns in schooling effectiveness than those that improve physical infrastructure and equipment. Another recent large-scale research project in the United States found that the wide disparities in achievement between black and white pupils attending different schools were almost entirely accounted for by the qualifications of teachers.

But improving the quality of teacher training requires more than imparting new pedagogical techniques. Several surveys have shown that many teachers do not feel responsible in any way for their pupils' failures. Instead, they believe that learning abilities are innate, so they tend to ascribe failure primarily to a pupil's low intelligence, lack of work or family background. These teachers regard their task as merely transmitting knowledge, rather than guiding pupils through a learning process.

Such attitudes among teachers are often intensified by poor working conditions and the lack of any professional framework through which they could exchange experiences and learn from their peers. Also, teacher morale and salaries are low in many countries, which does not encourage them to seek to improve their skills.

Any systematic effort to reduce school wastage should include measures to enhance the skills and working conditions of classroom teachers, especially those who teach in the early grades where repetition is greatest. Both preservice and in-service teacher training should aim to equip teachers with a variety of practical strategies for helping pupils learn in a timely fashion.

Teachers need to master pupil-centred approaches that recognize that each pupil has specific learning needs and requires a particular set of interventions. Various strategies can be employed to upgrade teachers' skills and attitudes and their capacities to introduce new curricular materials and teaching methods.

A number of countries, such as the Philippines, have found that school attendance can be improved and wastage reduced by organizing school calendars so that pupils in rural areas are not expected to attend school during planting and harvest seasons when their families need their labour. Similarly, the hours of the school day can be set to take account of the fact that some pupils, especially girls, must perform household chores.

Classes that include pupils of different ages have been found, under certain conditions, to be an effective way of dealing with the fact that pupils develop at different paces, especially during the primary school years. When teachers have been trained to manage such classes and to take advantage of the instructional possibilities inherent in such diversity, they often find that retention becomes unnecessary.

A considerable body of literature demonstrates the advantages of "frontloading" educational services to make sure that pupils get off to a good start in their schooling and build a strong base for future learning. A study in Madagascar, for instance, found strong correlations between pre-school education and lowered school wastage rates. A study in Mexico estimated that preschool education produced a 19 per cent improvement in performance on mathematics tests among the children of poor families.

In most developing countries, however, early childhood education is still considered to be a luxury and most such programmes are located in urban areas only. They are often considered by the personnel and the parents as a downward extension of schooling. Consequently, the personnel are not always sensitive to the developmental needs of pre-school children and force them prematurely into routine reading and writing.

Well-designed early childhood development programmes have proved to be effective in helping pupils from poor families to acquire some of the cultural attitudes and school-readiness skills that children from more affluent families learn in their homes.

It is important, however, that such programmes be carried out by competent personnel with special training. Instructional methods should aim to awaken children's interest in learning rather than to push them to early acquisition of formal academic skills.

The high rate of repetition in Grade 1 suggests how important it is for pupils to get off to a good start in their schooling. The selection, competence and behaviour of teachers responsible for the entry grade should be a priority in efforts to combat wastage. School administrators would do well to assign the best teachers to work with the beginning pupils.

A number of countries have found ways to put more resources, including teaching time, into the early grades. One approach is to provide remedial measures for chronic repeaters. Brazil's State of Saõ Paolo, for example, has developed an anti-wastage strategy that consists of creating accelerated classes for repeaters at two levels (Grades 1 and 2 and Grades 3 and 4) with the aim of rapid promotion to the higher level.

Intensive study in small groups and a belief in the pupils' innate possibilities are the hallmarks of this strategy, which targets the counties and schools with the biggest age-range per grade.

An estimated 10 per cent of all pupils have significant difficulties in learning at school. Children's disabilities and other learning difficulties may result from a number of factors: those within the child but also environmental factors such as poverty or lack of stimulation and school-related factors such as lack of good instructional materials, and inappropriate teaching and assessment standards.

The very concept of 'special needs' has thus widened to include all children who are failing to benefit from school for whatever reasons. Special education is no longer a marginal issue and is now more commonly referred to as inclusive education or the 'one school for all' approach.

School teachers need to be prepared for this shift in approach through preservice and in-service training. Certain prevalent attitudes towards disabilities also need to be reassessed so that schools can meet the learning needs of all the children in a community together.

Teaching aids, including textbooks, are scarce in many schools in developing countries. Faced with inadequate budgets that must cover teachers' salaries first, many ministries of education have little funding left to spend on textbooks and supplies. Yet numerous studies have demonstrated that the availability of textbooks is one of the major contributors to effective learning.

A 1997 UNESCO study on sustainable book provision points out that only a handful of industrialized nations possess both the technology of publishing and the knowledge and research to sustain a publishing industry. With few exceptions, developing countries, are poorly equipped to produce good quality learning materials. Consequently, they continue to import textbooks, but often in too small quantities, which is a costly way to alleviate some of the symptoms, rather than deal with the source of the problem – the absence of a publishing industry of their own.

Even when educators in these countries develop suitable educational materials, they often do so with little awareness of the professional skills needed to publish and distribute books at a reasonable cost. The promotion of national publishing industries is a promising strategy to enable countries to produce and disseminate suitable learning materials for their schools, as well as to more towards the wider goal of education for all, by creating and supporting a culture of reading.

Attaining the goal of Education for All requires overcoming the gender gap in primary schooling that characterizes most developing countries. To do so, it is necessary to understand the causes of the gap. Most societies make a clear distinction between men's roles and women's roles, and the latter often lie outside the mainstream of economic activities. One result, especially in rural communities, is that the education of girls is considered less important than the education of boys. Where the practice of child marriage continues, girls are withdrawn from school at puberty or are never enrolled. A study in Sierra Leone on the impact of the economic crisis on girls' education showed that parents chose to cut costs by withdrawing daughters before sons from the school.

With few exceptions, boys tend to be enrolled in school at significantly higher rates than girls in all developing regions and they then complete the primary-school cycle in larger numbers. However, a closer look at the data shows that once girls are admitted to school, their dropout rate is no higher than that for boys. This suggests that strategies to remove the gender gap should concentrate on getting more girls into school in the first place.

Various measures have proved effective in increasing girls' enrolment, such as waiving or reducing school fees for girls, supplying free textbooks, providing stipends for girls, offering flexible school hours and establishing childcare centres for the young siblings of girl pupils. To encourage the enrolment of girls, programmes in Pakistan and Niger give girl pupils a take-home food ration. Such incentives tend to encourage regular attendance and reduce drop-out.

In some cultures, the location of schools and their physical facilities influence girls' access to education. Building schools close to girls' homes, providing separate sanitary facilities and constructing boundary walls can encourage parents to send their daughters to school. Some countries have found that girls' enrolment and performance improve if they can attend single-sex schools. Bangladesh, Chad, India, Pakistan, Senegal and Yemen have made special efforts to build new classrooms for girls. Similarly, in some rural areas and traditional communities, girls' enrolment tends to increase when there are women teachers in the school.

In the long term, education itself can help close the gender gap. Curricula that convey positive images of girls and women contribute to removing gender biases and harmful attitudes towards women. Educated women are better equipped to exercise their rights and educated men are more considerate and ready to regard women as equals. Enlightened public policy can hasten reaching a critical mass of educated men and women who truly understand the importance of educating their sons . . . and daughters.

Whereas drop-out rates are often affected by social and economic forces beyond the control of educators, decisions on whether or not to promote pupils to the next grade are generally made by teachers. Repetition rates are thus a matter of educational policy and practice.

Unfortunately, decisions on repetition are sometimes taken for reasons that have little to do with the presumed educational benefits. A study on school wastage in Bahia, Brazil, found that such decisions are often made by teachers in a haphazard and discriminatory manner. Considerations such as dress codes, speech and social status frequently entered the picture. In other cases, retention – and even expulsion –were used to punish pupils considered to be inattentive, or insufficiently motivated or otherwise unco-operative.

In formulating promotion policies, school authorities would be well advised to survey the research literature first. A significant body of research indicates that the negative effects of repetition largely outstrip the expected benefits.

One study by the International Association for the Evaluation of Educational Achievement, for example, found no absolute relation between retention policies and overall pupil achievement. It noted that pupils in the Scandinavian countries and Japan, which have done away with grade repetition, typically perform well above the international average on comparative examinations. However, it should also be noted that several countries that at one time or another had policies of automatic promotion later abandoned them.

Panama and Puerto Rico decided to do away with automatic promotion when they discovered that too many pupils were leaving school lacking sufficient skills. Moreover, opposition to automatic promotion is strong among members of the teaching profession who, like most people, are reluctant to give up practices that have been followed for many years. This opposition is sometimes reinforced by broken promises of additional resources for remedial measures to help pupils promoted automatically despite their scholastic under-achievement.

Moreover, evaluation of pupils' achievement should be continuous, with the aim of detecting and compensating learning difficulties rather than selecting pupils for promotion. In Malaysia, for example, where automatic promotion is practised in the nine grades of primary and lower secondary education, each school assesses the achievement of its own pupils. There is also a national test each year for pupils in Grades 3 and 5, the results of which help teachers to make a better evaluation of their pupils' achievement and to compare it with the performance of pupils in other schools.

Some countries have taken a compromise position and permit repeating only at certain strategic points in a child's education. For example, Botswana allows repetition only for Grade 4 pupils who do not score sufficiently high on an achievement test and for Grade 7 pupils who do not gain admission to secondary school.

It is important to recognize that neither automatic promotion nor retention policies, by themselves, can solve the problems of children who experience difficulty in learning. Pupils who move on to the next grade without having mastered material at the previous level are likely to have trouble learning the new subject matter, too. Pupils who fail to grasp material presented in a particular manner and setting are not likely to have much more success by going through an identical experience a second time. In both cases, the more effective approach would be to provide specific teaching interventions that address the particular learning needs of each pupil.

Educators and policy-makers need first to identify the predominant causes of drop-out and repetition in their particular situation and then devise appropriate solutions, which may need to target particular grades, geographical areas, communities, and disadvantaged groups. Such decisions will be more soundly based when a suitable data collection system is in place, which can then provide feedback once the corrective measures are under way. Any attempt to reduce school wastage must be comprehensive and systematic in order to deal with its multiple causes. Some aspects of wastage, notably high repetition rates, can be addressed through changes in educational practice that are largely under the control of educational policy-makers. Other components, such as dropping out, are rooted mainly in economic and social conditions external to the school. Addressing them requires working with members of local communities as well as with political and other leaders. It is thus incumbent upon teachers and school administrators to make their fellow citizens aware of the cost to families and to society when children are excluded from school or fail in school.

Developing Curriculum for Functional Literacy

The definition of 'functional literacy' varies from place to place and with types of tasks. Some experts consider that a minimum of six years are generally needed to make a person functionally literate. In its simplest sense, a functionally illiterate individual is one "who cannot engage in all those activities in which literacy is required of his group and community and also for enabling him to continue to use reading, writing, and calculation for his own and the community's development". This definition, worked out by UNESCO for statistical purposes, provides an elementary context for our discussion.

In fact, the roots of functional illiteracy lie not exclusively in schools or school system but are spread far and wide in society, according to a report published by the International Bureau of Education (IBE). Describing the definitional issue, IBE report sums up: "Recent movements in Australia, Canada and the USA, as also in the Federal Republic of Germany, France and some other European countries, tend to show that there is no single definition of functional literacy, that its meaning varies across countries and even within countries depending on the specific context in which the term is used, and that the literacy needs change and grow as the society becomes more industrialized and as the daily tasks of a general and vocational character become more complex. As a consequence, estimates of the extent of functional illiteracy vary according to the definitions used and the kinds of functions accepted as evaluative criteria."

A distinction is sometimes made between absolute illiteracy and functional literacy. In industrialised countries the percentage of absolute illiteracy is considered much lower than that of functional illiteracy. Small percentages of functional illiteracy as well as absolute illiteracy can be traced in practically every industrialized nation, and this situation is likely to continue in future.

Despite universalized primary and basic level education in advanced countries, a small percentage of children as well as adults still fail to acquire basic literacy skills and functional competencies. In developing countries, on the other hand, absolute illiteracy is a dominant phenomenon.

Varied and multiple factors such as unfavourable home environment, economic pressures, shortage of timely guidance, unhealthy environment in the neighbourhood, not just the education department of a country, are assumed to be responsible for this predicament.

In developing countries, functional literacy is treated as part of a literacy continuum, not as a separate phenomenon. Usually, the stage of post-literacy and continuing education is expected to lead to basic/functional education depending on the extent to which conditions are favourable. The problem of basic/functional illiteracy in developing countries is thus both widespread and severe. Also, there is a close connection between poverty and illiteracy. People who are illiterate also happen to be very poor. It is demonstrated conclusively that the countries with the lowest levels of literacy are also the poorest economically. Women and children are especially vulnerable to the vicious circle of poverty and illiteracy.

The question of basic functional illiteracy has been a matter of global concern for several years, and this problem has attracted attention of various world agencies, commissions and institutions. In 1987, the United Nations General Assembly adopted a resolution (40/104) proclaiming the year 1990 as international Literacy Year (ILY). Two years before that the General Conference of UNESCO adopted a resolution (2.2) at its 23rd session concerning International Literacy Year and the follow-up activities to be organized under UNESCO's leadership in cooperation with other UN agencies.

The World Conference on Education for All held in March 1990 in Jomtien, Thailand, was a historic inter-agency initiative of this kind. Jointly sponsored by the United Nations Development Programme (UNDP), UNESCO, UNICEF and the World Bank, the Jomtien event has, by issuing a call upon nations on all continents, made the world community aware of a major crisis confronting education. The Geneva Conference on Education in 1990 was a major international follow-up programme of the Jomtien Conference.

Studies indicate that the number of adult illiterates in the world has increased from 890 million in 1970 to 949.5 million in 1985, and the UNESCO estimates for 1990 then showed only a slight decrease to 948.1 million due mainly to the decrease in the number of illiterates in developed countries. So far developing countries are concerned, the number of illiterates has in fact increased. In 1990 more than 400 million school-age children in developing nations were not attending school. In terms of school level, 132 million were of primary school-age and 274 million were of secondary school-age. The present state of affairs indicates that almost 1.5 billion children and adults are either illiterates or on the way of becoming so in the near future. This trend is likely to continue as population explodes on a continuous basis.

Another point of concern is the huge disparity between men and women in terms of their literacy status. Inequality in education between men and women has been most pervasive in developing countries. Presenting part of a global picture, the IBE report clearly states: "The disparity in literacy rates between women and men, rather than declining, is gradually growing. In 1970, the female share of global illiteracy was 61.0%, in 1985 it was 62.8%, and according to estimates for 1990 it is moving close to 63.5%. In some countries illiteracy among women is double that of men. Similarly, both in percentage terms and in absolute numbers of illiterates, there are sharp disparities among regions, among nations within regions, and among urban, rural and remote areas within nations. In most of the forty-two least-developed countries a majority of the adult population is illiterate, as poverty and illiteracy are inter-locked in a vicious circle. In some of these countries, illiteracy among women is more than 80%. "

UNESCO estimates for 1990 clearly indicated that the number of illiterates will reach 948.1 million. Of these, 916.6 million potential learners are in developing countries and only 31.5 million in developed countries, excluding those categorized as functionally illiterate.

A report of the Independent Commission on Population and Quality of Life (ICPQL) published in 1996 states: "The full potential of education is today far from being realized in almost all countries. In developing nations the right to basic education has not been met for 1.3 billion adults and children. The primary challenge for the next two decades, then, is to fulfill the right to education for all those who have not had access to it (including those who failed the first time round). Meeting the challenge will require a profound transformation of educational systems and approaches so as to adapt them to the rapidly changing needs of societies as well as to the opportunities offered by technological advances."

Many local, national and international organisations and institutions are extremely concerned about the present state of literacy. Presenting a scenario to describe how illiteracy is having negative impacts on individuals in developing communities and societies, the ICPQL report further says: "Literate people find it hard to grasp the full impact of illiteracy. In a world operating on written laws, rules, and instructions, being illiterate is a severe handicap when participating in decisions affecting life: it is tantamount to disability, affecting every aspect of living. It confines job opportunities to the most menial and low-paid tasks. It means being unable to read instructions on a packet of seed, a tin of powdered milk, or an oral contraceptive. It means being unable to read newspapers, street signs, warning signs. It means the inability to check legal rights, an inability to check if a title or deed is faulty. And it means being exposed to fraud and expropriation."

Additionally, confusion over targets and timetables for achieving primary education for all has not at all helped the cause of literacy. At a time when relentless and concerted efforts and initiatives in the eradication of illiteracy are needed, such confusion with respect to targets has checked the momentum of literacy education programming. The world movement against illiteracy is a race against time and therefore no opportunity should be lost.

Describing the confusion over targets and timetables for literacy achievement, the ICPQL report puts it succinctly: "But serious slippage has occurred with respect to targets and commitments set earlier by the international community to ensure universal, primary education. According to the Second UN Development Strategy adopted in 1971, for example, universal enrollment was to be achieved by 1980. By the time of the World Conference on Education for All (in Jomtien, 1990) the deadline had been pushed to 2000—although this referred to completion of schooling. The World Summit for Children (1990) adopted a more formal target for universal enrolment by 2000, but reduced completion of target to 80 per cent. The International Conference on Population and Development (1994) then rolled back the target another fifteen years (2015) [International Conference on Population and Development, 1994] This confusion in targets clearly begs an authoritative reconciliation."

The ICPQL report adds: "The Commission recommends that UNESCO and other qualified organizations jointly adopt, as soon as possible, an effective Strategy of Education for All by the year 2010. The adoption of such a strategy will be conditioned, of course, by the introduction of any alternative educational policy, one complementing or supplementing the efforts of the formal educational system. Preparations should begin immediately, by naming the decade 2001-10 the Decade of Universal Basic Education."

This explains that the situation of educational deprivation among both children and adults facing many developing, particularly least developed countries, is one of grave concern. Maximum efforts are needed to translate basic/functional literacy education for all into a reality. Various developments in this area over the past few years indicate that, despite commendable efforts by various national and international agencies including the UNESCO, little progress has been achieved in expanding literacy to those who need them most. One reason why consistent efforts are lacking is that estimates of the extent of literacy have varied according to kinds of functions accepted as evaluative criteria. Moreover, where literacy opportunities exist, excessive concern over quantity has led to deterioration of overall quality. Next, we will examine the question of appropriate and effective curriculum for literacy.

Curriculum Development

The debate over 'core curricula' is perhaps one of the longest running in the history of education. Yet very little progress has been achieved in this area of vital concern. Until recently, very little or no debate has taken place on how to deliver literacy. Unfortunately, most literacy providers have assumed that learners learn the same way within the traditionally fixed timeframe, and that instruction must follow the traditional teacher-centred format with learners congregating at a specific time in a specific location. As Gattas and Eger says: "The basic style of education has not changed in hundreds of years, yet it is becoming clear that people learn differently; some learn better in the morning, some at the night, some are more oral, some visual, some tactile."

In most cases, curriculum has remained a list of topics to be covered with little attention to conceptualization and learning strategies. In some cases, traditionally designed curriculum lends itself to a linear sequence of neatly packed lessons with little flexibility and opportunity left for re-design and innovations.

Describing a type of traditional curriculum, McKenzie observes: "In many cases, the curriculum is a list of topics to be covered with little attention paid to concepts, generalizations or learning strategies. This kind of curriculum lends itself to a linear sequence of neatly packaged lessons presented by the teacher. The role of information in such a curriculum is very tightly defined as something akin to processed food. Five hundred years of history are boiled down into a mere 500 pages of text. The textbook keeps only the most important facts. Even so, there is never enough time to get through it all. It's like rolling boulders up a steep hill."

Arguments against traditional curriculum design and development are gathering momentum in many different ways. Some authors believe that distance curriculum system needs more and better focus in the new learning-teaching environment. Perraton lists four research questions of wider interest in distance education, one of which is directly related to curriculum development. These are:

a) What guidance can be given to academic staff on the curricular content of their courses?

b) What guidance can be given on the instructional design and presentation of courses?

c) How can we demonstrate the legitimacy of distance education and design a system that will enhance that legitimacy? And

d) How can we justify the use of resources on distance education?

Although referred to the development of an expanded programme of distance education at the tertiary level, these questions are of crucial significance for both primary and secondary education, including literacy education at a distance. All these need to be explored considerably, but the question of curricular concerns is the heart of both traditional and distance education.

Perraton notes that classifications of human learning guiding curricular matters are often arbitrary and that it is difficult to finalise our discussion for the inclusion or exclusion of any particular subject within a particular curricular domain. Unfortunately, as Perraton says, 'there is little in the distance-education literature to help us, as it has tended to concern itself with means rather than ends'. A lack of discussion of curricular issues in the literature has not helped solve the 'hard practical problems of course design'. In fact, the question is not of shortage of literature per se, but of lack of focus on curricular concerns.

Various perspectives on curriculum and its important component— course design—have been expressed by different authors and writers. Some view that the course design should move from the teacher-centred to other or learner-centred alternatives. Others emphasize on an approach derived from a constructivist theory of learning which determines similar objectives for the curriculum. This approach is worth-considering because it may, in some way, help design curriculum that is learner-centred.

According to Nisbet, 'constructivist theory', "rests on the premise that learners create their own knowledge, structuring it in their own personal way, in a search for meaning and understanding". This implies that learning involves a personal construction of knowledge. As Zimmerman and Schunk say, "Learning is not something that happens to students: it is something that is done by students". This suggests that curriculum should be designed with a view to encouraging and facilitating what the constructivist calls the learner's personal construction of knowledge. Others argue that resources should be concentrated more on the creation of high quality materials for a particular course(s) of study and less on testing of these materials. Some others concerned with curricular guidelines hold that they will work if and when they are backed by activity design, and that the current gap between curricular guidelines and activity design should be closed.

It is also observed that there is limited insight and innovation in materials development for education, and that there are too few experts involved in the development of educational materials. Whatever opportunities exist for using technology in learning, they are basically left underexplored and rarely applied. Some others stress on both the content and process of learning and remind that what a person learns and how he/she learns are equally important.

One of the characteristics of the current educational paradigm is to view curriculum as "the stuff" that is delivered to learners. The emerging paradigm raises questions about the efficacy of traditional curriculum and stresses on the rights of learners to have a voice in curriculum decisionmaking. Miller notes that new technologies can be seen as a tool that can help us "orchestrate broad curricular and institutional change".

However, new technologies have only enriched the teaching environment, they have done little to alter the basic assumptions on what the institution and curriculum are based, suggesting that technology, in itself, does not necessarily have an impact on the curriculum, nor does technology itself lead us to a learner-centred curriculum.

According to Miller, the important questions facing open and distance education today as we consider the curriculum are not, initially, questions about technology. They are issues of social purpose, of the role and goals of the learner, and the nature of knowledge in an information culture. Among the issues of social purpose raised by Miller can be included the question of the external efficacy of schooling, because "reviews of school curriculum suggest a considerable discrepancy between what is taught and what should be taught in terms of evident social needs". Miller further says: "The information revolution has resulted in several changes that force us to reconsider our basic ideas about learning and the curriculum. First, of course, it has greatly expanded the amount of information in our lives. This has had several effects. It has, for instance, democratised information: information is no longer the province of the scholar alone.....At the same time that it has been democratised, information has been devalued by the 'information explosion'. Information in itself does not grant one as much power as it used to....Instead, we are beginning to understand that real power rests in our ability to find, analyse, and use information critically to make decisions, solve problems, and respond effectively to new situations. These capacities become the explicit goals or outcomes of education, rather than the implicitly-understood by products of having knowledge about something. This is a dramatic change in how we understand the goals of education and the role of information. Second, the information revolution has turned the ideal of lifelong learning into an everyday necessity. Education is no longer a one-time, or even a two- or three-time, experience that prepares us for the rest of our lives. We are all lifelong learners. We've even begun to see our institutions as 'learning organisations'."

Miller relates to a media-rich learning environment in which different technologies are brought to bear on the goals of the curriculum itself. He notes that we are witnessing an atmosphere in which the technologies are integrated and the educational power of these technologies comes not from how one or the other allows us to achieve some specific goal, but from how we combine them to achieve a new kind of learning community. In addition, it is now possible to integrate technologies "in a seamless way so that learners can easily move receiving presentations to interacting with other members of the community to searching information". Consequently, we are now witnessing an integrated, seamless, user-driven multiple-media environment.

Curriculum Objectives

Learner-centred approach to curriculum designing is not a peripheral, but a crucial component of DE programming. Such an approach places great values on the relevance, functionality and quality of programme objectives and content of learning. As the IBE report says: "One of the most critical operational aspects in any literacy programme is to determine the objectives and content of learning, and to ensure their relevance and functionality as well as their quality. The chief reason why this particular aspect is so central and critical is that it is expected to take into account the learners themselves and their characteristics, their needs and problems, their occupations and pre-occupations, their age and prior experience, and the environmental setting in which they live. Such a learner-centreed approach was recently highlighted by the World Conference on Education for All."

The content of DE courses can vary widely between places, situations and objectives, and caution must be exercised while determining the content of such course(s). How to make distance courses relevant is a major question. The IBE report provides that curriculum developers may use the following checklist to assess and augment the relevance of objectives and content in their respective literacy programmes:

(a) *Locational relevance*: urban, rural, mountainous, desert area - characteristics of the locale: local environmental condition;

(b) *Occupational relevance*: agricultural, industrial, supplementary income generation, etc.;

(c) *Gender relevance*: for men or for women, or for both;

(d) *Familial relevance*: related to child care, family learning, children's education, population planning, family income;

(e) *Cultural relevance*: national and social events, local celebrations, religious practices, community characteristics, political set up;

(f) *Temporal relevance*: learning for immediate application or for long-term or future use, contemporary development and current news;

(g) *Universal relevance*: common needs for all human beings such as health.

(h) *Technological relevance*: new technological devices and their increasing use and application in daily life.

Curriculum Innovations

Acceptable curriculum innovations, according Jenkins, Inquai, Dodds, and Warr, constitute one of the four essential criteria for success in distance education programming. The other three are: suitable materials, teacher orientation, and access to school resources. Jenkins et al present the three major ways in which distance education curriculum innovations can take place:

(a) to diversify the curriculum by introducing new subjects

(b) to improve choice, by making a wider range of subjects available and

(c) to change the content and emphasis of the curriculum by teaching traditional subjects with a more practical slant.

Policy Issues

Literacy education should now be considered "an essential international policy issue which affects the social and economic viability of both developing and industrialized nations". Policy considerations play an important role in that they provide guidelines, and add perspectives and thoughts for future actions.

There is a lack of consistent research on the various aspects of curriculum development for literacy education. More research needs to be conducted to provide guidance to academic staff on the curricular content of courses related to basic/functional literacy education. New research should focus on both the role of the content and the importance of process in the curriculum system.

Traditional assumptions about curriculum need to be changed. We need to explore curriculum issues that derive from a changing focus on the purposes of literacy education. In fact, literacy curriculum means more than the literacy programme of studies. The curriculum for literacy should contain provisions that allow acquisition of skills and construction of knowledge through a variety of interactions between the learners, the learner and the teacher, and the learner and resources in the new communication environment. In fact, the suggestion for a "profound transformation of educational systems and approaches" made by the ICPQL report also means or implies a comprehensive transformation of the existing/traditional curriculum systems.

Curriculum design should move from the teacher-centred to other alternatives such as the one that is guided by a learner-centred approach. New opportunities for using technology in learning should be explored and applied with a view to designing and developing curriculum based on such a learner-centred approach. New technologies can serve as a tool that may facilitate broad curricular change. New curriculum initiatives should, for example, explore the ways in which learning occurs when learners make connections between their own experiences and the new information they are required to have in the learning process. Fortunately, with the help of new educational technologies a high degree of learner-centred flexibility can be introduced in the curriculum, responding to today's literacy needs and contexts.

Attempts should be made to diversify the curriculum by introducing new subjects, and to improve choice by making a wide range of subjects available. These subjects include health and hygiene, child care, population, environment, basic legal knowledge and civics, and the world of work. Furthermore, the introduction of a large variety of productive and incomegenerating and, among others, relevant vocational skills such as weaving, carpentry, handicrafts, vegetable gardening, mushroom growing, poultry raising, co-operative marketing, canning, etc., should continue to be in the curriculum in most countries for different groups.

Curriculum objectives and content should consider locational relevance, occupational relevance, gender relevance, familial relevance, cultural relevance, temporal relevance, universal relevance, and technological relevance. Shifting demographics are also transforming the learner body in developing countries from a relatively homogenous population into a multi-ethnic, multicultural mix of men and women, children and adults. The distance learners come, in many cases, from such a variety of ethnic and cultural backgrounds that curriculum developers will not be able to achieve good results without understanding (ethnically and culturally, for example) what the learners need most. Decisions about technology should not drive our decisions about the curriculum. It is learner needs assessment which should drive our curriculum decisions. Continuous efforts need to be made to help eliminate barriers that inhibit education and learning of the illiterates of disparate socio-economic levels, languages, ethnicity or cultures and varied learning styles and rates.

A few factors essential for the curriculum development and design are:

— recruitment of high-quality staff

— appropriate training of such staff

— thorough learner needs assessment

— efforts towards working in well-established teams e provisions for allowing teams plenty of thinking-time to re-draft and refine items and

— organization of teams working to a learner-centred set of design principles, which are frequently reappraised.

Developing comprehensive curriculum based in emerging realities can, in some cases, be costly. As growth in funding for existing and new literacy education programmes has diminished, several education institutions and system—both formal and non-formal —focused on literacy problems have had to adopt new strategies to attract scarcer resources. Such institutions and systems should now seek more collaboration with business and private sector in order to address literacy concern of the local, national and world communities.

Distance education curricula are typically arranged around Western rational, linear thinking and rewards those fieldindependent learners who are self-directed. This orientation may in fact be discouraging learners in some communities. Curriculum development should also be geared towards those learners who are field-dependent.

Studies have found that several factors are responsible for attrition in distance learning courses. Poorly designed courses may not enhance learner completion of courses or educational programme. Courses therefore need to be designed and developed with a view to motivating learners to complete their courses of study and the programme.

Absence of proper standards concerning curriculum may lead to major confusions in the learning-teaching process. Curriculum standards that describe what teachers are supposed to teach and learners are expected to learn should, therefore, be designed in order to "provide clear, specific descriptions of the skills and that should be taught to students". Accordingly, international literacy curriculum standards should be finalised to provide clear, specific descriptions of the skills that should be taught to the illiterate learners in developing countries. However, curriculum standards set at such a level should be flexible enough to incorporate typical national or regional characteristics, conditions and situations in developing countries.

6

Parents' Assessment of Child Education

The information provided formally to individual parents about the learning outcomes and progress of their children typically takes three forms: a written report, parent-teacher meetings, and, for some parents, reports on their children's performance in standardised tests. In most schools, both teachers and parents can discuss the progress of individual students at any time, at the instigation of either party.

Parents place a higher priority on receiving information about their children's progress than any other type of information they receive from schools. The majority of parents express a degree of satisfaction with the information that they currently receive, although they also believe that the process could be made more effective.

As in most overseas systems, Australian parents receive information on their children's progress through written reports (one to four times annually) from teachers, and through parent-teacher meetings. They also learn about their children's achievements through reports from external tests and examinations, work samples, tests that the students bring home from school and through homework and informal discussions with their children and with teachers.

The rationale for encouraging parents to be active partners in the education of their children is built on research findings that show parental encouragement and support for learning activities at home, and parental involvement in schools and classrooms, have a positive impact on children's learning. High levels of parental involvement have also been shown to be strongly related to increased student motivation.

Parent involvement is a term used to describe the various processes of parental and community input to schooling. Fullan distinguished between parent involvement in instructional and non-instructional contexts. Instructional involvement relates to parent activities that provide assistance in the classroom or with learning activities at home, such as homework.

Non-instructional involvement refers to participation in decision making, governance and community-school relations. Instructional involvement by parents has direct benefits on the learning outcomes for their children. Epstein has disaggregated the processes involved in effective parent involvement into the following components:

— parenting practices and home conditions that support the learning of children in school;

— assistance with learning activities at home;

— monitoring student progress and student programs;

— involvement at the school - including assisting with and attending school activities; and

— contributing to decision making and advocacy through organisations such as parent associations, and school councils.

An Australian study of school effectiveness sought views about the roles that parents have in effective schools. Parents indicated the following roles, in order of importance:

— taking an active interest in the learning of their children;

— being actively involved in schools;

— communicating with schools; and

— participating in school decision making.

Research on the participation of parents in governance and decision making provides no evidence of a direct relationship between the degree of parent involvement and student learning outcomes. It does, however, provide evidence of a number of indirect benefits, such as increasing the resources for the school as well as individual benefits for the parents who participate through the enhancement of their planning and management skills.

A particular aspect of parent involvement that is explored in a number of recent studies is the concept of parents as complementary educators or partners, with teachers, in the learning process. Parents as partners, with a shared sense of purpose with teachers, provide the basis for improving student learning.

The central characteristics of effective parent-teacher partnerships in education as follows:

— sharing of power, responsibility and ownership, though with each party having different roles;

— a degree of mutuality, that begins with the process of listening to each other and that incorporates responsive dialogue and 'give and take' on both sides;

— shared aims and goals based on a common understanding of the educational needs of children; and

— commitment to joint action, in which parents, students and teachers work together.

Broadfoot argues that, to be respected as partners, parents must have relevant information to enable them to support the learning of their children. She indicates that there "is a gap between what parents say they want to know and what they get". The Scottish study found that the information provided to parents by schools was focused on 'social events' and 'activities within the school'.

There was less focus on information about the core educational processes of teaching and learning, the curriculum offered, and homework strategies. As a result parents perceived schools to be unwilling to share information about the fundamental processes of teaching, learning and the curriculum, a finding supported by other research in the UK.

One study has analysed differences in satisfaction with the information received by parents from primary and secondary schools. It found that primary schools were perceived by parents to be better at providing information on teaching strategies and activities within the school, as well as general information about school activities. Parents with children in primary schools felt involved in developing a shared understanding with teachers about homework.

Secondary school parents perceived themselves to be less knowledgeable than primary school parents about how they could help their children with learning at home. The study found, however, that secondary schools were more effective than primary schools at communicating information about the curriculum and matters of discipline to parents.

Parents are very clear and consistent about what they want in terms of the substance of reports on their children's progress. They want to be:

— kept well informed about their child's progress;

— given information about a range of different aspects of achievement covering all curriculum areas as well as information on social development and behaviour;

— informed about strengths and weaknesses (providing details of positive achievement only is not what either students or parents want, because it is not viewed by them as constructive); and

— provided with diagnostic assessments and constructive advice about how they can provide support for their children's learning.

Methods of assessing and reporting on student achievement are contentious matters among parents. Two distinct forms of reporting are common, narrative reporting, and reporting using grades and marks. Parents indicate the following areas of satisfaction and dissatisfaction with narrative reporting of student progress:

— They are satisfied with the detail of narrative reports. They believe they receive more information about their child from narrative reports than from other types of reporting.

— They are dissatisfied with narrative reporting when it is uninformative, vague, and ambiguous.

– They view narrative reporting as informative when it not only describes what the student has achieved, but includes evaluative comments about the level of achievement and expected levels of achievement.

— Other aspects of reporting provide marks or grades to indicate the level of a student's achievement.

School performance is defined as the average level of achievement of students in the school in the particular domain assessed, [eg. mathematics]... School effectiveness is defined as the relative level of performance of a school [for students of different backgrounds and levels of prior achievement] in a particular area of assessment.

In Kentucky, where schools receive incentive rewards for their effectiveness in meeting school improvement targets, schools serving disadvantaged communities are as likely as those in more advantaged communities to be effective. It is important that both the performance and the effectiveness of schools be assessed and reported. Focussing on performance only fails to recognise and reward schools that have lower performance principally because their intake of students had lower levels of achievement prior to their entry to those schools.

Parents place a higher priority on receiving information about their children's progress than any other type of information they receive from schools. Their interest is first and foremost in the development of their children and they use the information they receive to more effectively support their children's learning. Parents glean information about their children's progress from a range of sources, both formal and informal.

In Australia, reports from parents suggest that there is variability across the nation in the satisfaction of parents with the information they receive. The difference in satisfaction is not due to the State/ Territory or the type of education system in which children are educated, but to differences between schools. Parents in all States/ Territories, and in both government and non-government schools, provided evidence about the need to improve practices in reporting.

The majority of parents are satisfied, in general, with the information that they currently receive. A substantial minority of parents, however, detailed aspects of the reporting process and access to information about schools that did not meet their needs. A large proportion of parents overall indicated areas in which they seek improvement.

Many parents receive descriptive reports on student progress, as distinct from the rating or ranking approach described above. Descriptive reporting systems are more common in some systems than others, and are mostly linked to criterion-based outcomes approaches to curriculum. They are a relatively recent initiative.

Some schools also report to parents on the number of assignments not completed and some secondary schools include a comment from the pastoral care or year coordinator - or equivalent. This is usually a summary comment on the child and parents value these comments in the same way that they value interpretative comments on academic achievement.

Parents reported that they want information on the whole child, including academic, social, and emotional development as well as progress in extra-curricula , ctivities.8 They are particularly interested in knowing how their child is 'fitting in' or developing as a person. However, schools report relatively little of this information.

You need to know how your child is coping socially. You need to know how they interact with adults. You need to know whether they are confident enough learners to question... and whether they can take their learnings and adapt them in new situations. And a lot of it is learning in a social context.

Parents in schools with significant numbers of students from non-English speaking backgrounds (NESB) commented that their schools translated the reports for parents and provided interpreters at parent-teacher meetings. They indicated that criterion-based outcomes reporting had added to the workload of schools and were impressed with this support. English speaking parents also expressed concern in some instances, given their own difficulties with understanding reports, about how much NESB parents understood.

Most parents from non-English speaking backgrounds do not receive translated reports or have access to interpreters. Some parents with poor English language skills indicated that they would appreciate greater provision of translating and interpreting services.

Parents find systemic standardised testing programs that provide diagnostic information to be particularly useful. However, diagnostic information is of little use if schools do not know how to accurately interpret test results or fail to act to remediate any problems that are identified. Parents reported instances of learning problems identified in later years, which they subsequently discovered had been, or should have been, apparent from earlier test results.

Parents believe that standardised tests provide pressure for teachers and schools to maintain quality. They see teacher quality as integral to their children's progress and improvements in teaching as associated with improvement in student learning. Many parents, including those who support standardised testing, however, sounded a note of caution about their use.

They clearly do not want the tests to lead to unnecessary or excessive performance pressures being placed on students, particularly primary aged students, and they want safeguards to ensure that testing does not lead teachers away from a focus on teaching to a focus on testing.

Parents are information bowerbirds when it comes to knowing how their children are progressing. They use any information source, some not intended as formal reporting mechanisms, and sift and analyse the information to glean what may be useful to them. They build up a picture from multiple sources of information that give the same message.

Parents who visit the school frequently, particularly if they are classroom helpers, gain much information about their children's progress through those visits. As classroom helpers they are able to assess the standards of work in the classroom and make judgements about their child's achievements compared with other students and compared with specified standards.

Some parents use school open days (or nights) to learn about their children's achievements. These are scheduled occasions when parents are invited to the school and into classrooms to view children's work. Parents find these occasions useful for comparing their child's work with that of other students.

Homework is very useful in informing parents about how their children are progressing. Homework that is returned marked by teachers is even more useful. For many parents, homework provides an insight into what is being taught in classrooms. Homework is the only means that many have to assess on a regular basis how their children are achieving and progressing in the months prior to the first written report of the year.

Parents of secondary school students also find that homework tells them about how their children are progressing. They report, however, that secondary students are less forthcoming in showing them work. Homework assignments, particularly when the child involves the parents or discusses the work with them, is a common way that parents of secondary students learn about their progress.

Many parents report that teachers involve them formally in their children's homework practices. This most commonly involves having them sign off on their children's homework and has the effect of requiring parents to monitor the completion of homework. Most parents who reported this practice like it not only because it provides them with an entr...e that they might not otherwise get to their children's work, but also because it tells them that the school is organised about homework and monitors it. Parents mentioned that a weekly plan for homework is appreciated because it enables them to plan homework completion around family commitments.

Parents prefer to see homework that is relevant to the learning program. They do not like to see homework that they find meaningless 'busy work'. Parents use homework much like they use information from tests, to provide an insight into teacher and school quality.

Planned, meaningful and relevant homework practices send positive messages about school and teacher quality.

Parents find informal conversations with their children and with teachers a good source of information about their children's progress. They like to chat with their children, usually at the end of each day, about the day and what they did and what they learned.

Parents indicate that primary school children are generally more open than secondary children, but that all children can be encouraged to talk to their parents. If a child is having problems at school, he or she is less likely to talk about it easily with parents. Hence, parents say they cannot rely on their children alone to alert them to difficulties.

Parents also often find that visiting the school regularly puts them in a position to gather teacher comments in a less formal way. If they are regular visitors to the school and are known by teachers they find that they often have 'classroom door ' or 'canteen' conversations with teachers.

Parents noted a tendency, particularly among primary schools, to avoid facing or telling hard truths. They feel that teachers often couch negative comments in unclear or misleading language, or put comments on learning difficulties in a warm, encouraging and positive tone.

Parents who have children in both primary and secondary schools, particularly noted the contrast between the generally more precise reporting of the secondary school with 'fuzzy' reporting from some primary schools. Related to the lack of clarity is the inappropriate use of educational jargon. Parents criticised reports which they feel have not been tailored to their level of understanding. Many expressed a need to decode the language of reports.

Many parents believe that students already know the 'pecking order' in their classes. Others were uncomfortable about not being able to reconcile their need for an objective statement about the attainment level of their children with a strong dislike of competition and 'labelling'. This view is more common among primary school parents.

Some parents suggested that a system of recording students' results in tests (marks) would enable parents to see how their children were performing without them being ranked. Others were against any system of reporting based on standards established by individual schools, as they believed it could be inadequate or misleading for their needs, as one school's standard might not be high enough.

The comparability of school standards is critical when students change schools, move from primary to secondary school, or are preparing for post secondary schooling.

Parents also believe that a system based on state/territory level standards would expose under-performing teachers and put pressure on them to improve. The current situation enabled too much leeway for the teacher to set the standard, and that even when students were graded, it was only against the class-level standard. Under these conditions parents had no way of knowing whether the teaching standard at their school, and therefore the achievements of their children, were 'up to scratch'.

Reporting based on objective standards is likely to be more effective at detecting students who require additional support or referral to a specialist. A number of parents reported that too frequently student problems went undetected and 'slipped through the net' because there was little to alert teachers or parents to the problem.

Parents who are highly engaged with their children's learning often find considerable frustration when they receive a bland report, especially if it mainly features ticks or letter codes. They want something more substantial. They want reports that not only tell them what their children have achieved, but what they face next or need to do to improve. Importantly, they also want advice on how they, as parents, can help.

Parents' Role in Education

Parents rarely describe information only in terms of what is being communicated, they also describe it in terms of how it makes them feel as parents. They see school-to-home communication as an indicator of their relationship with schools. For example, if the communication is in warm, friendly, easily understood, jargon-free language and is comprehensive, parents perceive that the school welcomes them, is inclusive and values their role in their children's education.

If information or communication is dogmatic and aloof, sparing in content, or not in easily comprehended language, parents feel that the school views them less positively or undervalues their role in schooling. The information and how it is communicated signal schools' understanding of their relationships with parents. Parents' involvement in their children's education is a deeply emotional one. This is evident in the language parents use when talking about schools. They are not just interested third parties. They see themselves, not just their children, as having an integral personal relationship with the school.

The issue for schools in formulating communication policies is to understand and respond to this emotional engagement, to understand that anything that affects children is likely to have meaning for parents too. Children are central to their parents' lives. Many schools recognise this, but in the eyes of parents others appear not to do so, and are dismissive of the parent role.

Schools have particular challenges in regard to communication with parents from different cultural or educational backgrounds. The Aboriginal parents prefer to receive information in an informal communal setting. Parents who consider themselves to be less well educated are often intimidated by schools, at least initially. These parents want schools to recognise that providing information is not the same as informing them, and that sometimes the language used inhibits understanding.

The area where parents express the strongest need for further information is in improving their knowledge of curriculum, learning programs and teaching methodology. They want this knowledge to reinforce their understanding of at-school learning so they can assist their children at home, particularly if they are having difficulties.

Information nights are the main source of this information, however the timing of these sessions does not suit all parents, and they would like alternative times to be offered. Information nights also vary in quality. Whilst parents indicate some are excellent, others are said to be boring, repetitive and not specific enough to provide the information that parents find most useful.

There are some information needs that cannot be satisfied in information sessions. Many parents do not feel that they have the confidence, or knowledge to be able to assist students at home, especially where new teaching methods are involved, and would like practical training sessions. Mathematics and reading are the skill areas where primary parents, particularly, would like more knowledge of teaching strategies.

Secondary parents are much less satisfied than primary parents with the information they receive about teaching and learning. They receive little information about teaching methods and learning expectations. The adequacy of information about subject choice is a prominent issue for secondary school parents. Parents often have difficulty in accessing sufficient information to enable them to adequately understand the implications of particular subject choices. Many feel that schools have had little regard for the parent role in making subject choice decisions.

Secondary parents feel, in some cases, that they have been excluded from, or are given inadequate information relating to decisions about their children's subject choice. Subject choice is the area where secondary parents express strongest dissatisfaction. One mother said that she discovered the science program her daughter was enrolled in after a choice had been made without any parent involvement.

Choosing Schools

The primary purpose that parents cite for wanting to know about school achievement is to assist them to select schools for their children. Parents actively choose from among schools, particularly at entry to primary schooling and at the point of transition from primary to secondary school.

Parents are less likely to compare schools when selecting primary schools if they are satisfied with the school in which their children are currently enrolled. In government school systems where schools have been 'dezoned', parents are more likely to make an active choice of primary school, but the pool from which parents select is geographically narrower than the secondary pool.

Having made a choice of school parents rarely change unless there are very compelling reasons to do so. Pressure to change comes mostly from extreme dissatisfaction with how their children are progressing, a change of home location, or a need to change in Years 11 and 12 - in cases where the previous school caters only to Year 10.

A school can change from year-to-year depending on the teachers and the principal in the school and it's a big decision to make up your mind where you're going to send your children. Once you make that first decision, nine times out of ten you'll stay with [the school]. But if it's not working for a particular child - all children can be different in the family - then you have to be able to [seek out information on other schools].

Parents try to use information on school achievement to evaluate how well schools are meeting the needs of other children like their children and to seek assurance that schools are doing a 'good job'. Once their children have enrolled, parents judge the effectiveness of their school almost entirely on how the school is meeting their expectations for their own children's progress. That is, if their own children are happy and achieving according to parental expectations, they are less interested in the schools' achievements overall.

Those who ask for more accountability, a large minority of parents, want more information on how effective schools are in achieving their goals for students and want to know how well schools are meeting expected standards. Perhaps it would be good to find out at the end of the year if the teachers have done what they set out to do.

Some kind of common benchmarks for all schools would be helpful to parents. [It would] allow them to make informed comparisons. Schools should be assessed and monitored as to teaching quality, teacher competence. Parents express concern that the information they currently receive is not objective, that is it is made available for self-promotion purposes, or that it is inadequate.

Some parents have very specific requirements about the type of school that their children will attend. In these instances there is often not a lot that an individual school can do about its 'type', other than capitalise on its positive attributes. For example, parents may have a strong preference for schools in a specific sector - Catholic, independent or government. For other parents the first requirement may be that the school is single-sex.

Parents have quite strong views about their preferred size of school. Many value large schools, but others prefer their children to attend small schools. Parents who value larger schools choose them because they have more resources and expertise and are more likely to provide their children with a wider range of opportunities, such as extra-curricula programs. Parents who choose small schools do so because they provide a friendlier and more secure environment.

The location of a school is a consideration for parents when choosing a school. Rural parents regret that they have little choice, but report that they are generally satisfied with the local school.

Parents of primary school students usually consider the local school as their first option. It is usually the closest and most convenient school for parents and many believe through anecdotal evidence or previous experience of the school that the local school will be satisfactory for their children.

Provided local primary schools have a good reputation, parents will generally not look further afield. In this context, parents may choose among three or four local schools, where more than one school is viewed as serving the local area. By 'good' reputation, parents mean good student discipline, perceived high academic standards and a friendly environment. However, if children do not thrive in the local school, parents will seek an alternative.

Parents cast their net much wider geographically when choosing a secondary school. The location of the school is less important than for primary schools, but the availability of transport is an important consideration.

Some parents, however, were very happy with their relationship with secondary schools and described practices comparable with the best of those in primary schools. These parents do not accept that they need have a lesser role in their children's education in the secondary years. There are hardy parents who, in the face of secondary school resistance persist in taking an active role in their children's education. As one said, "You just keep knocking on their door".

Parents who are well-informed and active participants in their children's education are more likely to be satisfied with the quality of the school, the quality of the teaching and with their children's progress. Simple 'cause and effect', however, does not explain this set of relationships. Some parents who have been actively engaged in their children's schools have high levels of satisfaction with their children's progress. Others have stories to tell about significant disappointments they have had at some stage of their children's schooling.

In some cases, the additional useful and meaningful information that parents can access through a higher level of participation is reassuring to them. High levels of parent engagement and school-parent interaction can also place pressure on schools and teachers to maintain high professional standards. Parents thus have a role in 'keeping schools honest'. The converse of this may also be true, that schools with high professional standards value the role of parents in education and seek to keep them well-informed and involved. In some schools, however, active participation by parents is no guarantee that they will be provided with accurate and timely information that alerts them to any problems their children may be experiencing.

Parents have a vested interest in the outcomes of their children's educational development. Successful education is a prerequisite for work and access to careers. It is also an important vehicle for guiding children towards becoming happy, responsible, aware and productive adults who are able to contribute to, and participate effectively, in our society.

Parents who successfully manage their children's education oversee their children's development and take appropriate action to ensure that the needs of the children are being met. Other parents, those who are either too busy with other responsibilities or not sufficiently confident of their role in education, have a strong interest but are less active in managing their children's education. Both groups have a strong stake in knowing that their children's educational needs are being met.

Many parents view the roles of teachers and parents, respectively, as service provider and consumer. In this context, parents, either directly through fees or indirectly through taxes pay for a service and expect teachers and schools to account for their delivery of that service. Reports on student progress are the primary means by which parents learn about how well their children are progressing at school. The reports are the primary sources of information on which parents base future educational decisions.

There is a similarity in approaches throughout Australia- regular written reports and opportunities to attend parent-teacher meetings. However, there is considerable variation in the effectiveness of practices in meeting parent needs for useful, relevant and appropriate information. Both schools and school systems have a responsibility to ensure that best practice is adopted.

Schools need to review their reporting policies to ensure that they are providing parents with the information they want and communicating it in a manner that meets the needs of parents. School systems need to ensure that schools obtain advice and support to assist them to achieve best practice. In some instances additional developmental work and policy are also required. For example, additional professional development may be required or policies reviewed to assure systems that their policies are providing the framework necessary for best practice to be achieved. Underlying this should be recognition that effective reporting is intrinsic to successful learning.

The statements of best practice that follow have been derived from what parents indicate that they require and on examples cited by them of current school practices that they value. The national and international research literature analysed for this report provides a reference point from which to verify selected practices. The policies and practices of education systems across Australia provide the context for the discussion of how models of best practice might be achieved and what additional systemic support is required to assist schools to implement best practice.

The practices cited embody the fruits of developments that have led to current best practice. These practices incorporate the insights and initiatives of all groups with responsibilities to ensure that educational provision is of the highest quality- teachers, administrators, parents, researchers, and professionals in a number of other disciplines.

Managing Children's Educational Development

Schools and parents develop an effective partnership to support the learning of students. Schools that view the learning of students as the joint responsibility of teachers and parents in partnership are more likely to meet students' and parents' needs and produce better student outcomes than those that do not.

Achieving this goal will require a significant cultural change for many schools, while other schools have already achieved or are in the process of achieving this type of relationship with parents. Schools in which teachers do not have a partnership relationship with parents tend to view the education of students as the professional role of schools and their responsibility alone. They argue that parents should support them by fulfilling roles that schools ascribe for parents.

Schools in which teachers exhibit this latter approach often consider reporting on student progress as an obligation or a duty. They may also consider anything more than basic reporting as 'additional work'. Schools in which teachers view themselves as partners with parents in the education of children are more likely to approach the reporting process as a core element of the partnership and to focus not on what they are obliged to report to parents, but on what parents need to know in order for them to fulfil their role in the partnership.

Partnership implies mutual interests and goals with interlinked roles and responsibilities. Within a successful partnership parents have a broader, but quite distinct role from that of teachers. This is because they have a long-term interest in their child's education, whereas individual teachers are part of each partnership for specific periods of each child's education, and this may relate only to specific areas of learning, e.g., Science or English. Because of this, parents, and not teachers, are the principal managers of their child's lifelong education and are responsible for making choices that affect the outcomes of schooling.

Parents also have a major role in optimising children's learning in out-of-school time. This involves them in supporting and encouraging learning and the provision of additional resources or learning support. To be effective partners in managing their children's education they must have the information necessary to play their part. There are two implications for schools arising from this. The first is that parents must have accurate, useful, and timely information about their children's learning. The second is that parents must have access to opportunities that allow them to develop the skills, knowledge and confidence required to undertake their partnership role effectively.

The first implication is relevant to all parents, the second is particularly important to the large group of parents who require additional support and training to be confident educational partners with teachers. Parents most at risk are those who themselves did not have a successful experience of schooling. Such parents may not know how to take on an active partnership role, and may believe that 'teachers know best' and leave education to teachers. Others would like to take a more active role in their children's education but feel intimidated by schools and teachers.

Best practice in reporting to parents requires schools to be responsive to the circumstances of communities as a whole, as well as to individual families within communities. Schools exhibiting best practice go out of their way to be as approachable and welcoming as possible to all parents, frame their communications in language that all parents can readily understand, and provide advice to assist parents to support their children at home.

The attitude to parents of teachers and administrative staff in some schools results in frustration even though they may make considerable efforts to engage parents. Despite the best efforts of some schools, there still may be communication or cultural barriers inhibiting their relationship with parents, which may not be detected until schools listen closely to them.

For many schools, implementing a genuine partnership with the parent body and with individual parents will require a cultural change, but one that should produce a rich harvest for themselves and their students.

There is a high degree of congruence across all States/ Territories and all education systems about what parents consider most desirable in receiving information about their children's progress. Parents want to receive written reports at regular intervals. They want the written report to inform them about their children's standard of achievement, to include information about their children's progress in both academic and non-academic areas and to provide interpretative comments and advice about the meaning of the assessment for future development and progress.

Most importantly, parents want written reports to be in a format and language that they can readily comprehend. Parents also want to see and discuss examples of their children's work and marked tests. These enable parents to gain a practical understanding of the types of work that their children are undertaking.

Parents value, in particular, the opportunity to have a meaningful rather than a ritualistic discussion about their children's progress with teachers. They do not want a process that simply has the teacher reporting to them, but one that facilitates interaction and discussion about their children's progress. This includes teachers listening to what parents have to say about the learning of their children.

In addition to formal scheduled reporting, parents want to feel comfortable about approaching the school at any time for information about their child's learning or to raise a concern. Further, they want absolute assurance that schools will contact them immediately if there is a problem in relation to any aspect of their child's educational development and progress.

Bibliography

Armstrong, Alice, and Charles Casement, "The Child and the Machine: Why Computers May Put our Children's Education at Risk", Beltville, MD: Robins Lane Press, 2000.

Beattie, Catherine, "Technology & the Future of Schooling: Ninety-Fifth Yearbook of the National Society for the Study of Education". *Canadian Journal of Education*. v.22 (2), Spring 1997.

Bennet, Frederick, "Computers as Tutors: Solving the Crisis in Education", Sarasota, Fl.: Faben, 1999.

____________, "Computers, Classrooms and Cost-Cutting: High-Tech Backers Say Computers Help Deliver Education Efficiently", *Western Report*, v. 8 (46), Dec. 13, 1993.

Chouinard, Juel, "Book Review: The Child and the Machine: Why Computers Put our Children's Education at Risk", *Education Canada*. v.38 (4), Winter 1998-99, pp. 36-37.

Denny, Jason, Micheal Lindsay, and Sherman Riggers, "Computer Use in Elementary Education", April 10th, 2001.

McCraw, Phyllis A. and Jane E. Meyer, "Technology and Young Children: What Teachers Need To Know", April 10th, 2001.

Shade, D.D. and J.A. Watson, "Computers in Early Education: Issues Put to Rest, Theoretical Links to Sound Practice, and the Potential Contribution of Microworlds". *Journal of Educational Computing Research,* 1990. v.6 (4), pp. 375-392.

Van Scoter, Judy, Debbie Ellis, & Jennifer Railsback, "Technology in Early Childhood: How Technology Can Enhance Early Childhood Learning", April 10th, 2001.

Index